Presented to

_____

From

_____

Date

_____

Planted by the Water

Arnold R. Fleagle

CHRISTIAN PUBLICATIONS
CAMP HILL, PENNSYLVANIA

Christian Publications
3825 Hartzdale Drive, Camp Hill, PA 17011

Faithful, Biblical Publishing since 1883

ISBN: 0-87509-557-7
LOC Catalog Card Number: 93-74748
© 1994 by Christian Publications
All rights reserved
Printed in the United States of America

94 95 96 97 98   5   4   3   2   1

Cover Photo: © Chris Heisey
Cover Design by Robert A. Baddorf

CONTENTS

How to Use
Planted by the Water

Planted by the Water is conveniently arranged for daily devotional study and practical application. Each daily segment contains four primary sections:

SEED FOR TODAY
> The Scripture reading is taken from *The New International Version* and is designed to illuminate the daily theme.

LIGHT FOR TODAY
> This section provides an excerpt from an Alliance writer who has provided helpful commentary on the daily theme.

HYMN FOR TODAY
> A hymn selection, which is consistent with the daily focus, is included from *Hymns of the Christian Life*.

FRUIT FOR TODAY
> This section provides additional insight and suggestions to the reader so that the devotional truths may be applied in daily living.

Acknowledgments

*P*lanted by the Water is the result of a cooperative effort with the author by many friends and mentors who have contributed to its character and completion. I desire to thank the following people for their vital role in joining me to make my dream a reality: Harold Amos, Jeannie Brenneman, John Finley and Joel Smith.

I would acknowledge the leadership team at Christian Publications for their significant encouragement and expertise which were applied to this endeavor, including, Dr. K. Neill Foster, Marilynne Foster and Jon Graf.

Finally, I praise the Heavenly Father for my "faithful vine" and "olive branches." Faye, Matthew and Marc have been essential in my writing ministry and as "I grow in grace" they serve to enhance my experience exponentially.

Foreword

We have a problem in the whole evangelical community of our nation: a generic gospel. We are drifting toward a stripped down, bare-bones set of beliefs barely distinguishing us from the world, depriving us of the fullness of God's blessing, and providing us with a less-than-triumphant entrance to glory.

The situation is especially acute to The Christian and Missionary Alliance, which since its inception has taken a stand that the quality of life by faith in Christ should be "days of heaven on earth." It is to be life on a higher level made possible because He promised, "I have come that they may have life, and have it to the full."

Down through the years we have tried to make this promise accessible in teaching and preaching centered on Christ, who ransoms us from sin, recreates us in his image, delivers us from disease, and is coming again to take us to where He reigns in glory.

This four-point message is in danger of becoming like a four-wheel drive vehicle that loses its tires one at a time. No one really disputes the biblical soundness of sanctification, healing or the Second Coming. The problem is neglect, not rejection, but the result is the same: a down-sized salvation offering little more than a way to heaven.

One way to avert a breakdown is to keep repeating these biblical truths in a fresh way to each new generation of believers. Arnold R. Fleagle does just that in this devotional book.

Perhaps he is able to do so because, coming out of a different denominational background, he brings to the Alliance message a refreshing perspective. Too many of us are like veteran missionaries who, immersed for years in a foreign culture, no longer see its marvels so obvious to a new recruit.

With a combination of historic and contemporary writers brought together in a well-designed format, Dr. Fleagle accomplishes something quite unusual. Recognizing the short-spanned pace of our culture, he frames thoughts that make time stand still in our minds and hearts.

Bringing together a wide array of human needs and corresponding spiritual truths by various writers, he joins with those who, like the Apostle Paul, "have not hesitated to proclaim to you the whole will of God." It's the best way I know to spare us from a generic gospel.

Dr. David L. Rambo
President
The Christian and Missionary
Alliance

WEEK ONE: Day One
Theme: The Way

SEED FOR TODAY

They devoted themselves to the apostles' teaching and to the fellowship, to the breaking of bread and to prayer. (Acts 2:42)

LIGHT FOR TODAY

Conversion for those first Christians was not a destination; it was the beginning of a journey. And right there is where the biblical emphasis differs from ours.

Today all is made to depend upon the initial act of believing. At a given moment a "decision" is made for Christ, and after that everything is automatic. . . . We of the evangelical churches are almost all guilty of this lopsided view of the Christian life, and because the foundations are out of plumb, the temple of God leans dangerously and threatens to topple unless some immediate corrections are made. . . .

In the book of Acts faith was for each believer a beginning, not an end; it was a journey, not a bed in which to lie while waiting for the day of our Lord's triumph. Believing was not a once-done act; it was more than an act, it was an attitude of heart and mind which inspired and enabled the believer to take up his cross and follow the Lamb whithersoever He went.

A. W. Tozer
Born After Midnight

HYMN FOR TODAY

'Tis so sweet to walk with Jesus,
Step by step and day by day;
Stepping in His very footprints,
Walking with Him all the way.
Step by step, step by step,
I would walk with Jesus,
All the day, all the way,

Keeping step with Jesus.
*   "Step by Step"—A. B. Simpson*

FRUIT FOR TODAY

Jesus Christ called Himself "the Way" in John 14:6. His followers were described as those who belonged to "the Way" (Acts 9:8). Christianity was more than a decision, it was designed to be a path which wove itself through life on earth and then stretched itself into eternity. Christians need to take the "long view" of the faith that they embrace. Conversion is the first step but it leads to endless others, all making up the adventure of following Jesus.

Today, you will meet friend and foe, sunshine and shadow. Don't be too preoccupied with one or the other! There's so much more than one day when you serve Jesus Christ. Whatever happens to you this day, remember it is a long journey and He will not only lead you, but be your traveling companion all the days of your life!

WEEK ONE: Day Two
Theme: Time

SEED FOR TODAY

Be very careful, then, how you live—not as unwise but as wise, making the most of every opportunity, because the days are evil. (Ephesians 5:15-16)

LIGHT FOR TODAY

Two little words are found in the Greek version. . . . The two words *ton kairon* mean, literally, the opportunity.

It is intimated that there are not many such moments of opportunity, because the days are evil. Like a barren desert, in which, here and there you find a flower, pluck it while you can; like a business opportunity which comes a few times in a lifetime, buy it up while you have the chance. Be spiritually alert; be not unwise, but understand what the will of God is. "Walk circumspectly, not as fools, but as wise, buying up for yourselves the opportunity."

Sometimes it is a moment of time to be saved; sometimes a soul to be led to Christ; sometimes it is an occasion for love; sometimes for patience; sometimes for victory over temptation and sin. Let us redeem it.

A. B. Simpson
Days of Heaven on Earth

HYMN FOR TODAY

Redeem the time, for the days are evil!
It rings o'er the earth with its notes sublime;
'Tis the voice of God to His slumbering people;
Redeem, redeem the time;
Redeem the time, for the days are evil!
Let it ring through the world with its notes sublime;
The shadows are lengthening, the night is near,
Redeem, redeem the time.
    "Redeem The Time"—A. B. Simpson

FRUIT FOR TODAY

Someone has said, "Time passes." Another has replied, "Time stays, we pass on." The point is well taken—our time on earth is limited; it has a beginning and it has an end. Each day is another deposit of time that God has invested in our account. We are challenged not to spend it on ourselves, but to spend it wisely. We are deputized to look for opportunities and to seize them for the glory of God!

Today is the first day of the rest of your life. Here are three suggestions:

1. Pray that the Holy Spirit will enable you to invest your deposit profitably.
2. Praise the God who precedes time and who will postdate it.

3. Encourage *one* person today with a word of love or a deed of Christian compassion.

Psalm 90:10 informs you that 70 years is the normal span of days for your life. This equals more than 25,000 days, 600,000 hours, 36 million minutes and 2 billion moments!

WEEK ONE: Day Three
Theme: The Will of God

SEED FOR TODAY

Therefore, I urge you, brothers, in view of God's mercy, to offer your bodies as living sacrifices, holy and pleasing to God—this is your spiritual act of worship. Do not conform any longer to the pattern of this world, but be transformed by the renewing of your mind. Then you will be able to test and approve what God's will is—his good, pleasing and perfect will. (Romans 12:1-2)

LIGHT FOR TODAY

Some people seem to be certain that if they find God's will for them, it will include difficult tasks, great heartaches, unpleasant moments. They struggle between wanting to know His will and fearing what it may include. They speak of "surrendering to the will of God" as though that would be the ultimate accomplishment of submission. I find the very expression "surrendering to the will of God" distasteful. In a proper concept of the will of God, there should be no big struggle involving the ultimate raising of a white flag of surrender. A proper understanding of God's nature will help us to anticipate His will with joy. "Embracing the will of God" suits me better than "surrendering to the will of God." With joy I should hold it close to my heart as a priceless, untarnishing treasure, a gift from the hand of the Person who has more love for me than does anyone else in the universe!

I choose to believe God when He says that His will is "good" for me, and will be "pleasing" to me, and is "perfect" for me in every last detail. I do not mean to say that I believe every aspect of God's will for me will be beautifully pleasant. I only affirm that it is "good" and "perfect" and is ultimately "pleasing."

Charles W. Shepson
How to Know God's Will

HYMN FOR TODAY

I choose Thee, blessed will of God!
For in the circling of Thine arms,
The gladdest spring of joy I find;
Outside Thee fears and strange alarms.
I choose Thee, blessed will of God!
In Thee alone my heart can rest.
        "I Choose Thee, Blessed Will of God"
        —May A. Stephens

FRUIT FOR TODAY

The will of God requires sacrifice and self-denial. The symbol of our faith is not a pillow but a cross. However, the Bible is replete with those who "embraced the will of God" and experienced answers to prayers, triumphs in battle and moments of ecstasy and celebration. Moses embraced God's will and watched the parting of the Red Sea. Hannah embraced God's will and witnessed a "no vacancy" in her womb in the person of Samuel. David embraced God's will and leveled a giant gladiator named Goliath. Peter embraced God's will and preached a sermon which resulted in *3,000 converts.*

Today, as you embrace God's will you will encounter crosses and crowns. Bear fruit by trusting God that both have equal value as He uses them to accomplish His perfect will!

WEEK ONE: Day Four
Theme: Missions

SEED FOR TODAY

Do you not say, "Four months more and then the harvest"? I tell you, open your eyes and look at the fields! They are ripe for harvest. (John 4:35)

LIGHT FOR TODAY

Jesus addressed His disciples' misunderstanding of the harvest with a piercing rhetorical question: "Do you not say, 'Four months more and then the harvest'?" Rather than assuming they knew the right answer to this all-important matter, He mildly rebuked their slowness of heart while imploring their response: "I tell you, open your eyes and look at the fields! They are ripe for harvest."

No harvest can wait. It requires prompt action. In Cambodia, when the grain is ripe, the people live at the fields until the harvest is in. Several days delay could mean the loss of an entire crop due to unexpected late rains. So everyone goes to harvest—mothers and fathers, sisters and brothers, aunts and uncles, grandmothers and grandfathers. And they stay at the field until the harvest is in.

With regard to the higher work and world of lost men and women, we should be possessed by a holy impatience which will not wait on our convenience.

Cliff Westergren
Council Message, 1992

HYMN FOR TODAY

> *Work, for the night is coming,*
> *Work through the morning hours;*
> *Work while the dew is sparkling,*
> *Work 'mid springing flowers;*
> *Work when the day grows brighter,*
> *Work in the glowing sun;*
> *Work, for the night is coming*

When man's work is done.
       "Work, for the Night Is Coming"—Anna L. Coghill

FRUIT FOR TODAY

It's harvest time! The fields are ripe and white. According to John 4:35 the grain has changed from a yellow to a *white* hue (the Greek word for ripe is *leukos* from which we get such words as *leukocyte,* the scientific name for the *white* blood cell).

Today, ask the Lord for an opportunity to witness to someone who is "ripe and white grain." Ask Him to "open your eyes" and permit you to visualize a crop which stands ready for the picking. Even if that person does not allow Jesus Christ into his or her life, at the least you have been a sower and perhaps tomorrow will be the reaper. Praise the Lord for the individual He places before you!

Procrastination is not only the "thief of time" but the thief of eternal souls, which, tragically, should have been gleaned for the glory of God. There stands a tall, ripe, ready stalk of grain. Go ahead—it's an urgent task! Tomorrow it may be rotting on the ground!

WEEK ONE: Day Five
Theme: Healing

SEED FOR TODAY

By faith in the name of Jesus, this man whom you see and know was made strong. It is Jesus' name and the faith that comes through him that has given this complete healing to him, as you can all see. (Acts 3:16)

LIGHT FOR TODAY

The lame man by the instrumentality of Peter's words regarding Christ's name was given a ground for hope. Faith was born as he laid hold of that hope which rested on the power of Jesus Christ.

Jesus Christ is the Healer. Any physical touch must be His divine work. The Word of God sets this truth before believers as a reasonable expectation.

Those who seek healing need a correct understanding of the nature of faith. It is certainly the deep assurance that the promise will be realized because of the integrity, perfection, and power of God Almighty who makes the promise. But faith is more than assurance—it is obedience. The failure to comprehend this truth robs many Christians of the fruit of faith. True faith calls for a total commitment to the will of Christ.

The exercise of faith finally must be a comprehension of the triumph of Christ through His death and resurrection. The lame man believed the crucified and risen Christ for his healing. Since the atonement is the procuring cause of every redemptive benefit, faith in the efficacy of that atonement is essential to realized blessing.

Keith Bailey
The Children's Bread

HYMN FOR TODAY

There is healing in Jesus, the same as of old;
There is healing for all who believe and obey;
For the love and compassion that never grow cold
Are as able and willing to help us today.
There is healing in Jesus, healing for thee,
Healing for all who believe and obey;
There is healing in Jesus, healing for me—
Jesus, I take Thee for healing today.
   "Healing in Jesus"—A. B. Simpson

FRUIT FOR TODAY

The healing of the crippled beggar in Acts 3 reinforces the role of faith in the healing equation. Peter credits the appropriation of faith in Jesus Christ as an essential factor in the restoration of the man to normal health. Hope had a non-negotiable part in his healing. Hebrews 11:6 offers the correlation between faith and reward: "And without faith it is impossible to please God, because anyone who comes to him must believe that he exists and that he rewards those who earnestly seek him. "

Today, if you are praying that God will heal you or others that are afflicted, come before Him with a "reasonable expectation" that Jesus Christ *is* the Great Physician and that complete healing is possible through His power.

WEEK ONE: Day Six
Theme: The Fullness of the Spirit

SEED FOR TODAY
I am going to send you what my Father has promised; but stay in the city until you have been clothed with power from on high. (Luke 24:49)

LIGHT FOR TODAY

Jesus Christ wanted to take religion out of the external and make it internal and put it on the same level as life itself, so that a man knows he knows God the same as he knows himself and not somebody else. He knows he knows God the same as he knows he is alive and not dead. Only the Holy Ghost can do that. The Holy Spirit came to carry the evidence of Christianity from the books of apologetics into the human heart, and that is exactly what He does. You can take the gospel of Jesus Christ to the heathen in Borneo or Africa, people who could never conceive the first premise of your logical arguments, so that it would be totally impossible for them to decide on logical grounds whether Christianity was of God or not. Preach Christ to them and they will believe and be transformed and put away their wickedness and change from evil to righteous- ness and get happy about it all, learn to read and write and study their Bibles and become leaders and pillars in their church, transformed and made over. How? By the instant witness of the Holy Ghost to their hearts. This is the new thing that came, sir! God took religion from the realm of the external and made it internal.

A. W. Tozer
How to Be Filled with the Holy Spirit

HYMN FOR TODAY

Oh, how long we struggle!
Oh, how hard we try!
Helplessly we labor,
Helplessly we sigh
Till Thy Spirit gives us
Power from on high.
Power, power, power from on high,
Send us by Thy Spirit
Power from on high.
"Power from on High"—A. B. Simpson

FRUIT FOR TODAY

Christianity offers the believer more than a cosmetic overhaul; this faith promises "Christ in me." God has deposited His treasure in our earthen vessels. He is remaking us from the inside out. His Holy Spirit is changing us and rearranging us, designing us like the *master copy*, Jesus Christ.

Today, tell at least *one* person the difference you have detected since the Lord took up residence in your inner man. The culture majors on self-improvement, but offer your friend a more proven solution to a new life, the personal presence of Jesus Christ in a human heart. Then, affirm the difference by demonstrating the reality by the way you live your life. Present a "daily video" of "Christ in me."

WEEK ONE: Day Seven
Theme: Christianity

SEED FOR TODAY

For God was pleased to have all his fullness dwell in him, and through him to reconcile to himself all things, whether things on earth or things in heaven, by making peace through his blood, shed on the cross. (Colossians 1:19-20)

LIGHT FOR TODAY

Moreover, Christianity is not like other religions, merely a body of teaching, nor a round of ceremonies, nor is it even a code of ethics. It has, indeed, a body of teaching, which is the sum of revealed truth; it has ceremonial rites, which are divine ordinances; and it has a system of ethics, which is the highest in the world. But Christianity is more than a doctrine, more than ordinances, more even than morality. In fact, as the term is commonly employed, Christianity is not a religion. It is a life. Its essential element is the vital union of the soul with God. Apart from the person of the Lord Jesus Christ, not merely as the historic founder, but as the Supreme Fountain of a new life of Divine knowledge, love and power, Christianity would exist only in name. Take Christ from Christianity, and it would descend to the level of one of the religions of the world. Jesus Christ is the sum of all doctrine, the source of all virtue and the spring of all service. Hence, it is true that Christianity is Christ and Christ is Christianity.

George P. Pardington
The Crisis of the Deeper Life

HYMN FOR TODAY

This is my wonderful story—
Christ to my heart has come;
Jesus, the King of glory,
Finds in my heart a home.
Christ in me, Christ in me,

Christ in me—Oh, wonderful story;
Christ in me, Christ in me,
Christ in me, the hope of glory.
        "Christ in Me"—A. B. Simpson

FRUIT FOR TODAY

The marathon runner hits the "wall" at the 19.2 mile marker in the 26 mile race. The runner must then get a second wind! The Lord Jesus Christ is our second wind, enabling us to break through the "wall" and move on to the finish line.

Today, you will meet obstacles and opposition. The competition may be the weather, a flat tire, a weary employer, an inattentive family member, maybe a disobedient child. You will face that obstacle—but not alone! You have a teammate! You are indwelt with the living Christ!

As you encounter the crisis, as you face the stressor, as you look into the eyes of your opponent, say to yourself, *the battle is the Lord's*. It really is, for He stands with you and works within you!

WEEK TWO: Day One
Theme: Prayer

SEED FOR TODAY

". . . Now, Lord, consider their threats and enable your servants to speak your word with great boldness. Stretch out your hand to heal and perform miraculous signs and wonders through the name of your holy servant Jesus."

After they prayed, the place where they were meeting was shaken. And they were all filled with the Holy Spirit and spoke the word of God boldly. (Acts 4:29-31)

LIGHT FOR TODAY

No matter what our stature or status, we have the authority in the family of God to pray the prayer of faith, that prayer that can engage the heart of God and that can meet God's conditions of spiritual life and victory.

Our consideration of the power and efficacy of prayer enters into the question of why we are a Christian congregation and what we are striving to be and do.

We have to consider whether we are just going around and around—like a religious merry-go-round. Are we just holding on to the painted mane of the painted horse, repeating a trip of very insignificant circles to a pleasing musical accompaniment?

Some may think the path of the religious carousel is a kind of progress, but the family of God knows better than that. We are among those who believe in something more than holding religious services in the same old weekly groove. We believe that in an assembly of redeemed believers there should be marvelous answers to prayer.

We believe that God hears and actually answers our praying in the Spirit. Let it be said that one miraculous answer to prayer within a congregation will do more to lift and encourage and solidify the people of God than almost any other thing.

A. W. Tozer
Tragedy in the Church

HYMN FOR TODAY

> *Heavenly Father, we Thy children,*
> *Gathered round our risen Lord,*
> *Lift our hearts in earnest pleading—*
> *Oh, revive us by Thy Word!*
> *Send refreshing, send refreshing*
> *From Thy presence, gracious Lord!*
> *Send refreshing, send refreshing*
> *And revive us by Thy Word!*
>   *"Send Refreshing"—Daniel W. Whittle*

FRUIT FOR TODAY

The contemporary church of Jesus Christ can access the identical power that energized the first century church in the book of Acts.

The early church witnessed church growth at a breathtaking pace, watched thousands embrace Jesus Christ as Savior, felt the healing stream of Almighty God wash over a multitude of afflictions, bid good riddance to demonic forces as they fled from possessed humanity. A small group of men and women turned the world "right side up." Why?

The first Christians understood and activated the dynamics of prayer. Prayer was a primary weapon in their arsenal against the dark side. Paul declared in Second Corinthians 10:4, "The weapons we fight with are not the weapons of the world. On the contrary, they have divine power to demolish strongholds."

Today, use your weapon! Marvelous answers follow mighty prayer!

WEEK TWO: Day Two
Theme: Conformed to Christ

SEED FOR TODAY

And we know that in all things God works for the good of those who love him, who have been called according to his purpose. For those God foreknew he also predestined to be conformed to the likeness of his Son, that he might be the firstborn among many brothers. (Romans 8:28-29)

LIGHT FOR TODAY

What does it mean to be conformed to the image of Christ? When we begin to spell it out in everyday terms and bring Him into the throbbing life of the late 20th century, what do we find in this Man that challenges us to follow Him and be transformed into His likeness? In the God-Man we find those characteristics that comprise in their totality the summum bonum of human perfection. We find in Him meekness without a trace of weakness, we discover holiness without the sham of hypocrisy, we find humility detached from a grovelling servility, we find power without the blemish of pride or arrogance, we find suffering without the debilitating companion of self-pity. We find success without the grasping outreach of self-seeking. We see demonstrated in the daily life of this individual and in those final hours at Calvary a love that knows no limit. When we add all of this together we get some idea of the purpose of God in Christ when He speaks of conforming us to the image of His Son.

James E. Davey
The Riches of Grace

HYMN FOR TODAY

Oh, to be like Thee! blessed Redeemer,
This is my constant longing and prayer.
Gladly I'll forfeit all of earth's treasures,
Jesus, Thy perfect likeness to wear.
Oh, to be like Thee! Oh, to be like Thee,
Blessed Redeemer, pure as Thou art!
Come in Thy sweetness, come in Thy fullness;
Stamp Thine own image deep on my heart.
  "Oh, to Be Like Thee, Blessed Redeemer"
  —Thomas O. Chisholm

FRUIT FOR TODAY

In Psalm 8 David poses a question: "What is man that you are mindful of him, the son of man that you care for him?" (8:4). The answer to those twin inquiries is quickly supplied: "You made him a little lower than the heavenly beings and crowned him with glory and honor" (8:5). There is *one* word which translates the two English words, *heavenly beings*. That single word is *Elohim*, a Hebrew word which is sometimes translated "God." The answer could be framed in these terms, "You made Him a little lower than God."

The New Testament persists in portraying humanity's exalted potential by proposing the believer as being conformed to the image of Jesus Christ. Second Corinthians 3:18 describes this make-over as a process: "And we, who with unveiled faces all reflect the Lord's glory, are being transformed into his likeness with ever-increasing glory, which comes from the Lord, who is the Spirit." Nevertheless, the process is designed to result in an incredible product—we are to be facsimiles of Jesus Christ!

Today, don't aim too low, because the heavenly Father has great expectations for you! Someone has said, "Aim at the clouds and if you miss you may hit the eagle. Aim at the treetops and if you miss you may hit the ground." Aim high!

WEEK TWO: Day Three
Theme: Revival

SEED FOR TODAY

Every day they continued to meet together in the temple courts. They broke bread in their homes and ate together with glad and sincere hearts, praising God and enjoying the favor of all the people. And the Lord added to their number daily those who were being saved. (Acts 2:46-47)

LIGHT FOR TODAY

Common to every revival is its wonderful outburst of joy. There is no earthly joy that can compare with the ineffable gladness that wells up in the hearts of forgiven and restored people. When the agony of conviction, the awful sense of being abandoned, the grief and terror of sin are replaced with the blessed peace of forgiveness it is hard to find a worthy way of expressing it. To those persons caught up in a revival all the world seems altered; their hearts are lifted up, their faces are radiant. They are like those of the early church—they "eat their meat with gladness and singleness of heart."

And this joy is not confined to those sinning believers now restored nor to those newly converted. It especially fills the hearts of those believers who all along had mourned and sought God for the arrival of this day. This newborn gladness suffuses the atmosphere of the church service. The worship service throbs and glows with spiritual fervor. It is especially evident in joyful singing of hymns and spiritual songs, for this is the renewed man's way of best showing his feelings. Most of the church's best hymns and lyrics have their origin in the great awakenings.

L. L. King
As Many As Possible

HYMN FOR TODAY

Joyful, joyful, we adore Thee,
God of glory, Lord of love;
Hearts unfold like flowers before Thee,
Opening to the sun above.
Melt the clouds of sin and sadness,
Drive the dark of doubt away;
Giver of immortal gladness,
Fill us with the light of day.
    "Joyful, Joyful, We Adore Thee"—Henry Van Dyke

FRUIT FOR TODAY

Misery loves company, but company doesn't love misery. The

church must pulsate with celebration if it is going to attract those who are fatigued and battered by the world, the flesh and the devil. The Christian life permits the believer to rejoice in the sunshine and the shadows. Paul wrote repetitively about rejoicing from a Roman prison cell. History records that the Christians at Madagascar were singing joyfully after they had been thrown off the cliffs on their way to the forceful collision that would terminate their earthly existence. The contemporary church and its constituents must develop a healthy view of celebration and learn how the joy of God's people can impact the watching world.

Today, major on celebration and minor on complaint! Revival and renewal usher in waves of joy that splash those inside the sanctuary and those outside in the secular society. Tony Campolo wrote a book with this intriguing title, *The Kingdom of God Is a Party*. Don't just serve up vanilla Christianity! Sprinkle some joy into the menu of your life!

WEEK TWO: Day Four
Theme: Christian Intensity

SEED FOR TODAY
I have been reminded of your sincere faith, which first lived in your grandmother Lois and in your mother Eunice and, I am persuaded, now lives in you also. For this reason I remind you to fan into flame the gift of God, which is in you through the laying on of my hands. For God did not give us a spirit of timidity, but a spirit of power, of love and of self-discipline. (2 Timothy 1:5-7)

LIGHT FOR TODAY
   When my mother got up in the morning, she always built the fire in the kitchen stove and then stirred up the coals in the pot-bellied stove. These coals had been smoldering all night, so she only needed to stir them a bit, add a piece or two of kindling wood and shortly

the fire was burning brightly. At various times during the day, she would call me to "stir the coals." When she did, I knew to obey or else the corner where I was sitting reading my book would soon become quite chilly.

I thought about this one morning when I was reading where Paul told Timothy to "stir into flame" that which was in him. Before someone can stir into flame, there must have been an original fire built. Jesus brought that fire to our hearts when He saved us. When we obey and stir the flame, others will benefit from its warmth.

Delores Taylor
Women in God's Presence

HYMN FOR TODAY

> *Revive us again, fill each heart with Thy love;*
> *May each soul be rekindled with fire from above.*
> *Hallelujah! Thine the glory,*
> *Hallelujah! Amen;*
> *Hallelujah! Thine the glory;*
> *Revive us again.*
> "*Revive Us Again*"—William P. Mackay

FRUIT FOR TODAY

The practice of the laying on of hands is found in both the Old and New Testaments. This activity had many purposes: the blessing of individuals (Jacob and his sons, Jesus and the children); healing (Elisha and the Shunnamite's son, assorted usage by both Jesus and the apostles); and for the appointment and confirmation of people for specific tasks (the confirmation of deacons, the impartation of the prophetic gifts, the commissioning of missionaries). Timothy was Paul's apprentice and served as pastor to the church at Ephesus. He had participated in this special event (1 Timothy 4:14; 2 Timothy 1:6) and it had launched his pastoral career. However, this event, no matter how significant, was not sufficient to maintain his passion and power.

The fire flares up and it also dies down. Paul reminds Timothy that he is not just a passive observer in the pursuit of maximizing God's gift to him. He has an active role in "stirring up the gift" and "fanning the flame."

Today may be the perfect time to put some kindling on the fire, a prime time to stir up the smoldering coals. This may be a day to exercise your will to press forward, a day to pray not superficially but earnestly for the maximizing of your spiritual gifts. It may be time for renewal and rededication of your life to the Refiner's fire. Fire either purifies or destroys. Allow your God to do the former so that the gracious gifts He has placed within you may be productive and fruitful for Him!

WEEK TWO: Day Five
Theme: Evangelism

SEED FOR TODAY
The church sent them [Paul and Barnabas] on their way, and as they traveled through Phoenicia and Samaria, they told how the Gentiles had been converted. This news made all the brothers very glad. When they came to Jerusalem, they were welcomed by the church and the apostles and elders, to whom they reported everything God had done through them. (Acts 15:3-4)

LIGHT FOR TODAY
The evangelist's rejoicing eclipses that of all other achievements because of its eternal and divine dimensions. The Olympic athlete rejoices in a gold medal that he or she, after a brief time of ecstasy, tucks away in a trophy case and seldom thinks of.

Those who gain their satisfaction from riches, fame, political power and the best of earth's pleasures discover that these things are temporal. But the evangelist's exhilaration only increases with time and eternity.

Athletes admittedly find a measure of gratification in the thought that their feats were achieved through personal ability and strength. But how much more exciting to know that God by His Spirit working through our humble, imperfect witness has saved a person forever! How much more fulfilling to acknowledge with the psalmist: "The LORD has done great things for us, and we are filled with joy" (126:3).

Thomas Stebbins
Evangelism by the Book

HYMN FOR TODAY

O Master, let me walk with Thee
In lowly paths of service free;
Tell me Thy secret; help me bear
The strain of toil, the fret of care.
Help me the slow of heart to move
By some clear, winning word of love;
Teach me the wayward feet to stay,
And guide them in the homeward way.
"O Master, Let Me Walk with Thee"
—Washington Gladden

FRUIT FOR TODAY

Witnessing is not always easy, but it is essential! Human beings are communication channels through which the good news of Jesus Christ is transmitted to the world. You are one of those channels to communicate the message of redemption across the street or perhaps across the sea.

You don't always have to hit a home run. Perhaps your witness will move a person from first base to second base. Or, if they're in the middle of the diamond, you may succeed in advancing them to third base. And, if someone is standing on third base you may just bring them home to score a run for the "Redeemed Team!"

Today, share a word for Jesus Christ. In the next twenty-four hours, "punch a hole" in the darkness. If someone comes "home" you will rejoice, that lost person will be found and heaven will have a kingdom party! Luke 15:10 conveys this festive picture: "In the same way, I tell you, there is rejoicing in the presence of the angels of God over one sinner who repents."

WEEK TWO: Day Six
Theme: The Great Commission

SEED FOR TODAY
Then Jesus came to them and said, "All authority in heaven and on earth has been given to me. Therefore go and make disciples of all nations, baptizing them in the name of the Father and of the Son and of the Holy Spirit, and teaching them to obey everything I have commanded you. And surely I am with you always, to the very end of the age." (Matthew 28:18-20)

LIGHT FOR TODAY
"Go ye therefore, and teach all nations" (Matthew 28:19, KJV). It was His great manifesto as King. He was about to ascend to His throne. Before doing so He proclaimed: "All power is given unto me in heaven and in earth" (28:18, KJV). And with that proclamation He sent forth His ambassadors to call the nations of earth to His kingdom. They were to teach observance of all Jesus' commandments to the very end.

Jesus accompanied His commission with the promise of His providential presence. It is a presence that carries with it all the omnipotence of the Godhead. It is an unfailing presence that none can claim in its fullness if they are not obeying the command that precedes it.

Jesus' Great Commission has never yet been fully realized. It contemplates a worldwide evangelization so glorious and complete that no nation, tribe or tongue will be overlooked! It calls us to focus on the nations rather than on the isolated individual; unevangelized peoples should be the first object of our care. Nor are we to rest until this glorious gospel shall have been proclaimed in every tongue spoken by man. God wants representatives from every nation to herald the return of the Son of Man!

A. B. Simpson
Missionary Messages

HYMN FOR TODAY

Send the gospel of salvation
To a world of dying men;
Tell it out to every nation
Till the Lord shall come again.
Go and tell them, go and tell them
Jesus died for sinful men;
Go and tell them, go and tell them
He is coming back again.
    "Go and Tell Them"—A. B. Simpson

FRUIT FOR TODAY

God's plan of salvation is not parochial—it is panoramic. He has embraced the whole earth with eternal love. Second Peter 3:9 articulates our heavenly Father's all-inclusive desire: "The Lord is not slow in keeping his promise, as some understand slowness. He is patient with you, not wanting anyone to perish, but everyone to come to repentance."

If our vision is in focus we will have global vision. If we feel for lost men and women only a fraction of what God feels for lost men and women we will not allow the Great *Commission* to become the Great *Omission*!

The heavenly choir is a rainbow coalition as it is painted in Revelation 7:9: "After this I looked and there before me was a great multitude that no one could count, from every nation, tribe, people and language, standing before the throne and in front of the Lamb."

Today, celebrate your active role in the Great Commission and take inventory and implement a strategy to get involved. "A hundred thousand souls a day/ Are passing one by one away . . ."

WEEK TWO: Day Seven
Theme: Favoritism

SEED FOR TODAY

And masters, treat your slaves in the same way. Do not threaten them, since you know that he who is both their Master and yours is in heaven, and there is no favoritism with him. (Ephesians 6:9)

LIGHT FOR TODAY

There is no favoritism with God. The Bible very plainly declares it. But I think of Abraham, Jacob, Moses, David, Daniel, Peter, James, John—even Paul himself. Did not God choose these for special assignments and permit them to get closer to Him than the rank and file? Yes, He did. But that is the mystery of free will and predestination. A sovereign God knows in advance who has the capacity and the will to love Him supremely and to obey Him without reservation. There is no favoritism with the Lord. I may be a slave or a master, poor or rich, handicapped or perfect; at Calvary the ground is absolutely level. It is the disposition, the attitude that I bring to my relationship with God that determines how high I rise in the arms of faith.

Clearly, then, the next move is mine. However close or distant my past relationship with Deity, God is giving me new opportunity today—now—and maybe in the tomorrows—to draw near. The One who has no favorites makes an open, unconditional promise to me and to every one of His children: "Come near to God and he will come near to you" (James 4:8).

H. Robert Cowles
Prime Time

HYMN FOR TODAY

I am so glad that our Father in heaven
Tells of His love in the Book He has given.
Wonderful things in the Bible I see;

This is the dearest, that Jesus loves me.
I am so glad that Jesus loves me,
Jesus loves me, Jesus loves me!
I am so glad that Jesus loves me,
Jesus loves even me!
    "Jesus Loves Even Me"—Philip P. Bliss

FRUIT FOR TODAY

Have you heard the story of the man who paid $3,000 to have his family tree looked up and then paid $5,000 to have it hushed up? All of us possess skeletons in our closet. We all have Achilles's heels! We all have sinned and fallen short of the mark which God has set for us (Romans 3:23). Both sin and grace are equalizers!

The cross is able to plant us all on common ground. The princess and the prostitute, the banker and the bankrupt, the healthy and the handicapped, all fall into one category at the cross. There is no distinction. Galatians 3:28-29 presents a more positive version of equalization: "There is neither Jew nor Greek, slave nor free, male nor female, for you are all one in Christ Jesus. If you belong to Christ, then you are Abraham's seed, and heirs according to the promise."

Today, it is time to stop belittling ourselves and to look up to His wonderful grace. "Whosoever will" broadens the constituency of those who can access God's mercy and grace. "If any man" is a phrase that stretches the spectrum of the candidates who can experience God's ineffable love! He has set the table, paid for the meal and issued the invitation: "Come and dine!" He has no favorites!

WEEK THREE: Day One
Theme: Horizontal Ministry

SEED FOR TODAY

"Then the righteous will answer him, 'Lord, when did we see you hungry and feed you, or thirsty and give you something to drink? When did we see you a stranger and invite you in, or needing clothes and clothe you? When did we see you sick or in prison and go to visit you?'

"The King will reply, 'I tell you the truth, whatever you did for one of the least of these brothers of mine, you did for me.'" (Matthew 25:37-40)

LIGHT FOR TODAY

Jesus did not only preach and "win souls." He healed all kinds of broken bodies and fed needy people. Many publicans and harlots and outcasts found in Him a kind of "city of refuge." He had a solution for every strata of society. When in prison, John the Baptist began to doubt whether Jesus really was the Messiah. Jesus reassured him with the message: ". . . the blind receive their sight, and the lame walk, the lepers are cleansed, and the deaf hear, the dead are raised up, and the poor have the gospel preached unto them" (Matthew 11:5).

Christ walked the same streets as the outcasts; He ate with all kinds of "sinners." He lifted the bruised and crushed. He suffered for the suffering. He made the lame to leap and the dumb to sing. He ministered to every man and to every need. He offered help as "far as the curse is found."

Both the vertical and the horizontal are central in the life of Christ. Two beams made up His cross and they pinpoint the directions of His life. The one reaches up to His Father, the other out to men. His power was vertical—His ministry was horizontal. His feet were nailed (or tied) to the vertical beam; His walk was "from above" and always pleasing to His Father. His hands were nailed to the horizontal beam; with those hands He blessed little children and multiplied loaves and fishes for the hungry. He touched the sick and the blind. He never did anything but good—and was crucified for it!

Armin R. Gesswein
With One Accord in One Place

HYMN FOR TODAY

Sowing in the morning, sowing seeds of kindness,
Sowing in the noontide and the dewy eves:
Waiting for the harvest and the time of reaping,
We shall come rejoicing, bring in the sheaves!
"Bringing in the Sheaves!"—Knowles Shaw

FRUIT FOR TODAY

John Wesley declared, "Orthodoxy, or right opinion, is at best a very slender part of religion." Our faith must not only be flowing through our hearts and heads, it must travel through our extremities. Our arms, hands, legs and feet are to be instruments of His love and mercy.

Today, target a person in physical need and offer them assistance. Use your antennae to locate one who has just dropped her groceries or one who can't see to back out of a parking space. This may be the moment to take a pie to a neighbor in bereavement or to transport a sick person to the medical center.

As you carry your cross, don't neglect the horizontal beam which stretches out to a hurting humanity!

Praise the Lord at the day's end because you have extended Christ's love to a weaker brother or sister.

WEEK THREE: Day Two
Theme: Self

SEED FOR TODAY

For the grace of God that brings salvation has appeared to all men. It teaches us to say "No" to ungodliness and worldly passions, and to live self-controlled, upright and godly lives in this present age, while we wait for the blessed hope—the glorious appearing of our great God and Savior, Jesus Christ. (Titus 2:11-13)

LIGHT FOR TODAY

There is something more serious than coldness of heart, something that may be back of that coldness and be the cause of its existence. What is it? What but the presence of *a veil in our hearts?* . . . It is the veil of our fleshly fallen nature living on, unjudged within us, uncrucified and unrepudiated. It is the close-woven veil of the self-life which we have never truly acknowledged, of which we have been secretly ashamed, and which for these reasons we have never brought to the judgment of the cross. . . .

It is woven of the fine threads of the self-life, the hyphenated sins of the human spirit. They are not something we *do,* they are something we *are,* and therein lies both their subtlety and their power.

To be specific, the self-sins are these: self-righteousness, self-pity, self-confidence, self-sufficiency, self-admiration, self-love and a host of others. They dwell too deep within us and are too much a part of our natures to come to our attention till the light of God is focused upon them. The grosser manifestations of these sins, egotism, exhibitionism, self-promotion, are strangely tolerated in Christian leaders even in circles of impeccable orthodoxy. . . . I trust it is not a cynical observation to say that they appear these days to be a requisite for popularity in some sections of the Church visible. Promoting self under the guise of promoting Christ is currently so common as to excite little notice.

A. W. Tozer
The Pursuit of God

HYMN FOR TODAY

I will say "Yes" to Jesus;
Oft it was "No" before,
As He knocked at my heart's proud entrance,
And I firmly barred the door;
But I've made a complete surrender,
And given Him right of way;
And henceforth it is always "Yes,"
Whatever He may say.
I will say "Yes" to Jesus,
"Yes, Lord, forever yes.
I'll welcome all Thy blessed will
And sweetly answer Yes."
    "I Will Say 'Yes' to Jesus"—A. B. Simpson

FRUIT FOR TODAY

The culture in which we live programs us to major on *me*! "I Did It My Way" was a best-selling song which applauded the individual's right of self-determination and choice. "You deserve a Buick" has become an advertising success because it appeals to our desire to merit something special. The kingdom of God is not interested in self-actualization but Christ-actualization. This is a radical concept which is offensive to persons who have made their goals and their glory preeminent.

Today, reflect on the words of John the Baptizer: "He must become greater; I must become less" (John 3:30). The world would choke on this reality, but it is fundamental to the authentic Christian. Christians don't play leap frog with power and position! They follow their Lord's prescription: "Your attitude should be the same as that of Christ Jesus: Who, being in very nature God, did not consider equality with God something to be grasped, but made himself nothing, taking the very nature of a servant, being made in human likeness. And being found in appearance as a man, he humbled himself and became obedient to death—even death on a cross!" (Philippians 2:5-8).

WEEK THREE: Day Three
Theme: Missions

SEED FOR TODAY
And this gospel of the kingdom will be preached in the whole world as a testimony to all nations, and then the end will come. (Matthew 24:14)

LIGHT FOR TODAY
What is the impelling motive strong enough to send men and women into the dark places of the earth, among peoples alien in thought, manners, customs and life, to endure loneliness, homesickness, separation from children, heat, disease, frustrations, disappointments, ideals unrealized, and perhaps death? As we ponder the question, as no doubt many . . . have done, there are some reasons that emerge.

The first is a burning conviction that men and women are lost without Christ, and a sense of urgency that they must hear the gospel ere they die. These and a consciousness of Christian responsibility to give to others what has done so much for oneself are the basic impulses.

Then there is the categorical imperative of the divine command of the Lord Jesus to "Go and preach the gospel to every creature," which is taken to be unconditionally binding upon all Christians to be witnesses for Him either at home or abroad. The field is the world and to whatever part one is called one must obey.

Obedience becomes easy when a divine solicitude is implanted within the heart. There must be a consuming love for the Saviour and a love for the souls of those for whom He died, irrespective of their race or color. There must be a recognition of the fact that the whole world suffers from a universal disease and requires the universal remedy God has supplied which is available for all who will accept it and is equally efficacious for all.

J. H. Hunter
Beside All Waters

HYMN FOR TODAY

We've a story to tell to the nations
That shall turn their hearts to the right,
A story of truth and mercy,
A story of peace and light,
A story of peace and light.
For the darkness shall turn to dawning,
And the dawning to noon-day bright,
And Christ's great kingdom shall come to earth,
The kingdom of love and light.
> *"We've a Story to Tell to the Nations"*
> *—Henry E. Nichol*

FRUIT FOR TODAY

"The Whole Heart For The Whole World" was the theme of one church's missionary conference. Our "habits of the heart" reveal so many people with a very self-contained, parochial and narrow vision. There is an inclusive flavor to God's love that must be reflected in your love.

Today, as you read the front page of the newspaper and you are confronted with the tension and turmoil around the globe, *stop—* pray for some of the situations in those countries and intercede for the men and women who are ministers and missionaries in these "hot spots." It will enlarge your missionary vision!

WEEK THREE: Day Four
Theme: Discipline/Discipleship

SEED FOR THE DAY

When Pharaoh let the people go, God did not lead them on the road through the Philistine country, though that was shorter. For God said, "If they face war, they might change their minds and return to Egypt." So God led the people around by the desert road toward the Red Sea. The Israelites went up out of Egypt armed for battle. (Exodus 13:17-18)

LIGHT FOR TODAY

We are told here that the Lord led them not by the way of the Philistines, which was near, "but about through the way of the wilderness of the Red Sea." So we infer that God does not always lead us by the nearest way, and certainly not by the easiest way, as He calls us to Him. . . .

There are many other things about the way He led them which apply to us. The first was that He might have them apart with Himself and train them for the future. And so God has to take all His children apart to teach them. Our dear Lord had to go apart into the wilderness forty days before He began His ministry. Let us not wonder if we share His life. Moses had to go forty years apart before God could use him. And Paul went three years into Arabia, where he was separated to God, and then came forth to do his Master's work. . . . So, beloved, if you had an easy path you would become a coward and run away every time you saw a Philistine. The people that have no trials and discipline are just like this, they are soft and cowardly. And the one that God wants to make strong to undergo the journey to Canaan, He has to make hardy by discipline and training. He leads you by the hard way that you may be harnessed, may be trained as a soldier to fight the battles of your life, educated for your work by the very things you are going through now.

A. B. Simpson
Divine Emblems

HYMN FOR TODAY

Man may trouble and distress me—
'Twill but drive me to Thy breast.
Life with trials hard may press me;
Heaven will bring me sweeter rest.
Oh, 'tis not in grief to harm me,
While Thy love is left to me;

Oh, 'twere not in joy to charm me,
Were that joy unmixed with Thee.
     "Jesus, I My Cross Have Taken"—Henry F. Lyte

FRUIT FOR TODAY

Science tells us that when the oak tree encounters a storm, the soil around that tree is loosened, which allows the roots to sink deeper. This enables the durable tree to be stronger and more resilient. Many Christians are hammered out and shaped on the anvil of disappointment and difficulty.

In amateur wrestling there are three periods. The successful coach is aware that the third period demands an athlete with superb conditioning. He will prepare his wrestlers by strenuous training and exercise so that when the third period arrives, the wrestlers will be able to perform and defeat the opponent.

Today, when you have to take the longer road or encounter the thunderstorm, rejoice that in God's winning equation these are factors for success!

WEEK THREE: Day Five
Theme: Repentance

SEED FOR TODAY

When he comes, he will convict the world of guilt in regard to sin and righteousness and judgment. (John 16:8)

LIGHT FOR TODAY

Christians feel they must present the gospel in positive terms lest they create a negative image for Jesus Christ. Conversion thus becomes acceptance of Jesus Christ, with hardly a ruffle to that Adamic nature the Scripture calls flesh. Is modern man so fragile a creature that his conversion must be abetted with such conveyor belt ease?

What does Scripture say? Our Lord spoke of the Holy Spirit's ministry as including reproving or convicting the world of sin (John 16:8), the sin of failing to believe on Him. Paul told the Thessalonians that salvation came "through sanctification of the Spirit and belief of the truth." This sanctification is twofold in nature: being rent away from what we were and being set apart to become a child of God through the new birth, receiving His nature in order to accomplish His will.

Conviction and rending are terms of action. Fallen men see, through the Word of God and the work of the Spirit, what they really are and how desperately they need Jesus Christ. The Scriptures describe such a holy violence as repentance.

Donald L. Roberts
The Perfect Church

HYMN FOR TODAY

I've wasted many precious years,
Now I'm coming home;
I now repent with bitter tears;
Lord, I'm coming home.
Coming home, coming home,
Nevermore to roam,
Open wide Thine arms of love;
Lord, I'm coming home.
  "Lord, I'm Coming Home"—William J. Kirkpatrick

FRUIT FOR TODAY

The formula for salvation incorporates both repentance and reception. Jesus' initial message in the Gospel of Mark reinforces this thesis: "The kingdom of God is near. Repent and believe the good news!" (Mark 1:15). When Peter's great sermon on the Day of Pentecost convicted men (Scripture says they were "cut to the heart") his advice to them was "Repent and be baptized, every one of you, in the name of Jesus Christ for the forgiveness of your sins. And you will receive the gift of the Holy Spirit" (Acts 2:38).

We are much more adept at receiving God's gifts of grace than we are at repenting of our sins. However, *both* are essential to the fitness of our faith.

Today, is there any sin, stain or impediment in your life? Acknowledge it before the Lord! It is painful but also a prerequisite for the reception of His wonderful forgiveness and renewal. Conviction is part of conversion's fabric—repentance is part of redemption's fabric!

WEEK THREE: Day Six
Theme: I AM

SEED FOR TODAY
Moses said to God, "Suppose I go to the Israelites and say to them, 'The God of your fathers has sent me to you,' and they ask me, 'What is his name?' Then what shall I tell them?"

God said to Moses, "I AM WHO I AM. This is what you are to say to the Israelites: 'I AM has sent me to you.' " (Exodus 3:13-14)

LIGHT FOR TODAY
The Hebrew name for the Creator-God was "the Elohim." In the first chapter of Genesis, prior to the creation of Adam and Eve, the word Elohim was mentioned thirty-five times. Elohim is a plural noun, indicating to some scholars the presence of the Trinity during Creation. This name carries with it a sense of God's greatness and glory, His creative and governing power, His omnipotence and sovereignty.

In Genesis 2:4, however, where we begin to learn more about Adam and Eve, the name "Jehovah" is used for the first time. Jehovah is a God of moral and spiritual attributes. He is a God of righteousness and holiness.

Jehovah is to have a special relationship with people. He desires to commune with this man and woman He has created, to have fellowship with them, to enjoy them in a different way from the way He enjoys the animals and the rest of creation. . . .

Elohim is great and glorious; Jehovah is righteous and holy. Adam and Eve were created in God's image of greatness and glory *and* of righteousness and holiness.

It was against God's righteousness and holiness that Eve sinned when she listened to the serpent. Consequently, the greatness and glory God had given His creation were lost. A righteous Jehovah whose holiness was violated was forced to condemn unrighteousness—and to punish it.

So Eve had to leave the garden and enter a wilderness.

But the name Jehovah has another meaning. . . .

The name Jehovah is rooted in the Hebrew word *havah*, meaning "to be" or "being" or "I am becoming." As a child I was fascinated by those strange biblical words in capital letters—"I AM THAT I AM"—but I did not understand their meaning.

What a delight to discover that another translation of the name Jehovah is "I am becoming all that you need."

Joy Jacobs
When God Seems Far Away

HYMN FOR TODAY
> *The God of Abraham praise,*
> *Who reigns enthroned above;*
> *Ancient of everlasting days,*
> *And God of love.*
> *Jehovah, great I AM,*
> *By earth and heaven confessed;*
> *I bow and bless the sacred name,*
> *Forever blest.*
> *"The God of Abraham Praise"—Thomas Olivers*

FRUIT FOR TODAY
The choosing of a name in our time and culture does not hold the same significance as in other periods of history. For example,

the Puritans would label their children "Resolve" or "Persistence" so that a challenge would be intrinsic in the child's identity.

The Jews of the Old Testament placed a premium on the naming of their offspring. Hannah had been barren, but when God answered her prayer, she selected the name "Samuel," which means "asked of God." Rebekah's one twin came out of her birth canal holding on to his brother's heel, therefore, the boy was named "Jacob," which means, "he grabs the heel."

God has a number of names and titles. When He instructed Moses to inform the Israelites of His name, He intentionally conveyed His all-sufficient character by declaring, "I AM WHO I AM."

Today, when it happens, when you are short on patience, strength, love, tolerance, finances or whatever, access the incomparable I AM!

WEEK THREE: Day Seven
Theme: The Good Shepherd

SEED FOR TODAY

I tell you the truth, the man who does not enter the sheep pen by the gate, but climbs in by some other way, is a thief and a robber. The man who enters by the gate is the shepherd of his sheep. The watchman opens the gate for him, and the sheep listen to his voice. He calls his own sheep by name and leads them out. When he has brought out all his own, he goes on ahead of them, and his sheep follow him because they know his voice. (John 10:1-4)

LIGHT FOR TODAY

In Burkina Faso it is often the job of the young children to take the sheep and the goats out to the bush each day so that they can graze. Shepherd duty is something that adults avoid because it is considered to be the job of children or a slave. We usually see the children going out each morning with their flocks. They walk behind the flock and push them forward as they go out into the bush. Everything goes well until someone or something surprises the sheep. Then they become disoriented and scatter causing the children to run after them adding to the confusion. Eventually, the children, with much running and shouting, push them back together again until the next surprise or until the leader of the flock decides to turn aside into another field.

One day I heard the voice of an older man who was walking down the road. It was evident that he was talking to someone but I could not see anyone with him. Being curious, I went down to the window to see what was happening. Following along behind him was his flock of sheep and goats. If one started to stray he would speak to it and it would come back to the group. When a man on a bicycle passed him his flock did not scatter. A bush taxi passed and still his sheep stayed in rank. His flock knew him and his voice and wherever he went they did not scatter as did the flocks of the young children.

Jesus is our Good Shepherd and as long as we, His sheep, continue to listen to His voice and fix our gaze upon Him the surprises in our lives will not frighten and scatter us. We know our Shepherd and have confidence in His ability to lead us.

Wyman Nelson
Furlough Sermon

HYMN FOR TODAY

Saviour, like a shepherd, lead us,
Much we need Thy tenderest care;
In thy pleasant pastures feed us,
For our use Thy folds prepare;
Blessed Jesus, blessed Jesus,
Thou hast bought us, Thine we are;
Blessed Jesus, blessed Jesus,
Thou hast bought us, Thine we are.
  "Saviour, Like a Shepherd, Lead Us"
  —Dorothy A. Thrupp

FRUIT FOR TODAY

Every day each of us chooses a voice to follow. The world issues many siren calls to "Come, follow me." Jesus issues the same call—"Come, follow me" (Matthew 4:19).

It is crucial that we understand that when we choose our leader, we also choose our destiny and the consequences that are attached to that journey.

Today, Jesus appeals to us as the "Good Shepherd" who has died for His sheep. Reaffirm Him as your leader! Reaffirm His footprints as your guide! Then, your destination is a landscape of green pastures and still waters.

WEEK FOUR: Day One
Theme: The Cross

SEED FOR TODAY

When you were dead in your sins and in the uncircumcision of your sinful nature, God made you alive with Christ. He forgave us all our sins, having canceled the written code, with its regulations, that was against us and that stood opposed to us; he took it away, nailing it to the cross. And having disarmed the powers and authorities, he made a public spectacle of them, triumphing over them by the cross. (Colossians 2:13-15)

LIGHT FOR TODAY

The Christ-event is central to our faith, and central to the Christ-event is the cross. It was at Calvary, nearly 2,000 years ago, that Jesus reconciled humankind to God. At the unbelievable price of His shed blood and broken body, believers receive cleansing and redemption. It is Christ's atoning sacrifice that sets people free from death, giving victory and life everlasting to those who believe. We must never forget the centrality of His sacrificial death. The Lord calls us to continually remember His death until He returns to take the church into God's eternal glory!

It is far too easy to underemphasize the place of the cross in our faith. The "name it and claim it" cults place an emphasis on success and abundance. They treat suffering as sin and focus more on receiving than giving. It is difficult to reconcile the cross to such a theology, so they often overlook or underemphasize it.

. . . As we rejoice in resurrection power, we must not forget the atoning death of Christ on Calvary.

Terry Wardle
Exalt Him!

HYMN FOR TODAY

I must needs go home by the way of the cross,
There's no other way but this;

I shall ne'er get sight of the gates of light,
If the way of the cross I miss.
The way of the cross leads home,
The way of the cross leads home;
It is sweet to know, as I onward go,
The way of the cross leads home.
　　"The Way of the Cross Leads Home"
　　—Jessie B. Pounds

FRUIT FOR TODAY

Don't worry about finding the cross in your life. If you follow Him it will find you. And when you encounter it, the challenge is to receive it as a complement to the degree that you are sharing in your Savior's plan and purpose. It is *inevitable* that you will have a cross to bear! You will have scars on your faith! Like the Velveteen Rabbit, your Christianity is not real until it has some chewed up hair, some twisted fur, some bare spots.

Today, if you and I are going to follow Jesus Christ, to walk in His steps, then the cross will be a recurrent landmark on our pilgrimage. "To this you were called, because Christ suffered for you, leaving you an example, that you should follow in his steps" (1 Peter 2:21). The cross for the Christian is a plus sign.

WEEK FOUR:　Day Two
Theme: Atonement

SEED FOR TODAY

For he chose us in him before the creation of the world to be holy and blameless in his sight. In love he predestined us to be adopted as his sons through Jesus Christ, in accordance with his pleasure and will—to the praise of his glorious grace, which he has freely given us in the One he loves. In him we have redemption through his blood, the forgiveness of sins, in accordance with the riches of

God's grace. (Ephesians 1:4-7)

LIGHT FOR TODAY

A Scottish shepherd had a ewe that had lost her lamb, while another lamb was motherless. Vainly he tried to make the lambless mother accept the motherless lamb. She would have nothing to do with it, but pushed it rudely from her with cruel and heartbroken anger, because it only reminded her of the one she had lost.

At length a sudden solution occurred to him. He took the skin of the dead lamb and with it covered the living one, and then he brought it to the offended mother. Instantly her whole manner changed to the tenderest affection. She welcomed the little one with a mother's tenderness, caressed it, washed it, fed it from her bosom, and treated it henceforth as if it were the very lamb she had lost.

So He hath made us accepted in the Beloved. So He receives us even as His own dear Son. . . .

In His redemption, Christ purchased for us certain rights. To us they are the free gifts of God's mercy, utterly undeserved by us. To Him they are simply the fulfillment of a covenant whose condition He has met, and whose promises He is entitled to claim to the full.

A. B. Simpson
Wholly Sanctified

HYMN FOR TODAY

Christ has for sin atonement made,
What a wonderful Saviour!
We are redeemed! The price is paid!
What a wonderful Saviour!
What a wonderful Saviour is Jesus, my Jesus!
What a wonderful Saviour is Jesus, my Lord!
"What a Wonderful Saviour"—Elisha A. Hoffman

FRUIT FOR TODAY

The price tag of your atonement, your "at-one-ment," was beyond logic or reason. Jesus Christ took what *you* deserved in order that you might have what *He* deserved.

The sons and daughters of Adam have become the sons and daughters of God. His fractured body and His spilled blood qualified you to have *your* name written in the Lamb's book of life (Revelation 20:12-15). You are loved!

Today, when your self-esteem slides or someone devalues your worth or you simply do something which qualifies as a new "Murphy's Law," remember this fact of your faith: you are loved!

WEEK FOUR: Day Three
Theme: Jesus' Sacrifice

SEED FOR TODAY

You see, at just the right time, when we were still powerless, Christ died for the ungodly. Very rarely will anyone die for a righteous man, though for a good man someone might possibly dare to die. But God demonstrates his own love for us in this: While we were still sinners, Christ died for us. (Romans 5:6-8)

LIGHT FOR TODAY

One day Rev. Ha Hieu Ho, a Vietnamese church growth director, was visiting a certain tribal village. The people were slashing the jungle, clearing a plot of ground for planting their crops. After piling on the jungle cuttings, they burned the brush and planned to rake the ashes into the ground to help in their planting.

On this particular day as they burned the brush, they noticed a strange phenomenon. A big blackbird kept flying over the fire and gradually the bird came lower and lower peering intently into its flames. Suddenly, the bird nosedived right into the heart of the fire. The head of the village was heard to exclaim, "That crazy bird, it dove right into the fire and burned to death."

That night, after eating his supper and going to bed, he pondered the reason for that bird's crazy behavior. The next morning, after the ashes had cooled, he went into the field and with a stick, he sorted out the ashes, until he discovered the carcass of the dead blackbird, now burned to a crisp. He stooped over, picked up the bird, and to his amazement, he found three baby birds under the bird's wings. They all had survived!

The mother bird had left her nest the previous morning to search for food for her babies. In her absence, the men had cut down the branch where her nest was located. When she returned from her hunt she circled over the fire until she detected her nest and the plight of her babies. Immediately, she dove into the flames and covered her babies under her wings. She sacrificed her life to rescue others from a terminal plight.

And this is what God did for us. He saw our plight from above and sent His Son to offer His life that we might be salvaged from sin and doom.

Spence Sutherland
Furlough Sermon

HYMN FOR TODAY
Alas! and did my Saviour bleed?
And did my Sovereign die?
Would He devote that sacred head
For such a worm as I?
At the cross, at the cross where I first saw the light,
And the burden of my heart rolled away,
It was there by faith I received my sight,
And now I am happy all the day!
"At the Cross"—Isaac Watts
(Refrain by Ralph E. Hudson)

FRUIT FOR TODAY
Oxygen is essential to many living organisms. It is released into the environment by a process known as *photosynthesis* whereby plants capture sunlight and use it to make energy. As this process occurs, oxygen molecules are released into the air.

Love is essential to human organisms. It is released into the world by a process we might call *Christsynthesis*. People capture the *Son*'s light and use it to make spiritual energy. As this process occurs, love molecules are released into the earth's environment!

The Son's light reached a man named Paul and he penned this affirmation: "For Christ's love compels us, because we are convinced that one died for all, and therefore all died" (2 Corinthians 5:14). This is the process of *Christsynthesis*!

Today, develop the process of *Christsynthesis* in your own life.

WEEK FOUR: Day Four
Theme: Taking Up the Cross

SEED FOR TODAY
Then he said to them all: "If anyone would come after me, he must deny himself and take up his cross daily and follow me. For whoever wants to save his life will lose it, but whoever loses his life for me will save it." (Luke 9:23-24)

LIGHT FOR TODAY
God's solution to man's fall and marred image was not to make him a "superman" through redemption, but to restore man after the image of Christ in full humanness. Therefore, an incipient elitism that cultivates a "holier-than-thou" image is unChristlike, and a spirituality that seeks to escape human reality by divine power is unbiblical.

The cross is a reminder that human life is genuine and eternal. In the cross earth and heaven are bridged for the highest state of development which God designed for human life. To live for one's own ego is to create one's own prison, but to live for Christ and His kingdom opens earth to heaven with all its resources. To deny one's self and to take up the cross and follow Christ is the call of the gospel as we repent of our sins and accept Christ as Savior. But to come to terms with the self-life means crucifixion of one's privileges and prerogatives even as it was for Jesus who sanctified Himself to the Father without reserve. . . .

But the cross has a lifeside as well as a deathside. Christ Himself becomes our Sanctifier and baptizes us with the Holy Spirit to fill us with Himself and make us instruments for His glory. Man's highest freedom and fulfillment comes about through an obedience that is of divine enabling. God expects believers to accept their humanness as Christ did—in unreserved and voluntary submission through the living Spirit of God.

> Samuel J. Stoesz
> *Sanctification: An Alliance
> Distinctive*

HYMN FOR TODAY

> *Must Jesus bear the cross alone
> And all the world go free?
> No, there's a cross for everyone,
> And there's a cross for me.
> The consecrated cross I'll bear
> Till death shall set me free,
> And then go home my crown to wear,
> For there's a crown for me.*
>> "Must Jesus Bear the Cross Alone?"
>> —Thomas Shepherd

FRUIT FOR TODAY

The Christian journey is filled with paradoxes. Statements are inscribed in the New Testament which appear false and contradictory but in reality are bedrock truth! The last is first, the greatest is the humble servant and the life that loses itself in God is the winner!

Today, don't look at the obvious with too much confidence—it may not be the actual. To deny oneself and follow Jesus Christ is the surest way to treasure and triumph. To die to oneself is to encounter the eternal Christ and to accrue eternal life! The most restricting actions often translate into the most liberating experiences. Decide to find and travel the road which leads to real reward. Live the paradox!

WEEK FOUR: Day Five
Theme: The Power of God

SEED FOR TODAY

Say to God, "How awesome are your deeds!
  So great is your power
  that your enemies cringe before you.
All the earth bows down to you;
  they sing praise to you,
  they sing praise to your name."
          Selah

Come and see what God has done,
  how awesome his works in man's behalf! (Psalm 66:3-5)

LIGHT FOR TODAY

It is hard for us sons of the Machine Age to remember that there is no power apart from God. Whether physical, intellectual, moral or spiritual, power is contained in God, flows out from Him and returns to Him again. The power that works throughout His creation remains in Him even while it operates in an atom or a galaxy.

The notion that power is something God separates from Himself and tosses out to work apart from Him is erroneous. The power of nature is the Presence of God in His universe. This idea is woven into the book of Job, the Wisdom books, the Psalms and the Prophets. The writings of John and Paul in the New Testament harmonize with this Old Testament doctrine, and in the book of Hebrews it is said that Christ upholds all things by the word of His power.

We must not think of the power of God as a wild, irrational energy coursing haphazardly through the world like a lightning strike or a tornado. . . .

The power of God, then, is not something God has; it is something God is. Power is something that is true of God as wisdom and love are true of Him. It is, if we might so state it, a facet of His being, one with and indivisible from everything else that He is.

A. W. Tozer
Born After Midnight

HYMN FOR TODAY

I sing the mighty power of God,
That made the mountains rise;
That spread the flowing seas abroad,
And built the lofty skies.
I sing the wisdom that ordained
The sun to rule the day;
The moon shines full at His command,
And all the stars obey.
"I Sing the Mighty Power of God"—Issac Watts

FRUIT FOR TODAY

"Omni" has become a popular term in our culture. There is a car named Omni. The magnificent athletic complex in Atlanta, Georgia, is known as the Omni. Omni means *all*. It appears in the word *omnipotent*, which means all-powerful. There is only one personality who is worthy of the description—God!

God's power is not divorced from His purpose. Don't be fearful that He will overdo it and destroy you. He is also *omniscient*, all knowing. Don't speculate on Him deserting you for He is also *omnipresent*—always present. What a mighty God we serve!

Today, access the omnipotent God. When you do, the ordinary becomes extraordinary, the mundane becomes majestic, the impossible becomes possible (remember the loaves and fish!).

WEEK FOUR: Day Six
Theme: The Power Jesus Promised Us

SEED FOR TODAY

He said to them: "It is not for you to know the times or dates the Father has set by his own authority. But you will receive power when the Holy Spirit comes on you; and you will be my witnesses in Jerusalem, and in all Judea and Samaria, and to the ends of the earth." (Acts 1:7-8)

LIGHT FOR TODAY

Our word "dynamite," which represents one of the most powerful substances known to modern science, is derived and practically transferred with scarcely a change of sound or spelling, from the Greek word used for "power" in this and many other texts in the New Testament. The Holy Spirit is the mightiest dynamic force of the spiritual world. Indeed, He is the One supreme spiritual Force, and He is promised to the believer and the Church as the Source of their spiritual power.

There is nothing we need more than power. Man, once the lord of nature, is now one of the weakest of all earthly beings. The human babe is more helpless than the infant progeny of any living creature, and often requires almost a quarter of a lifetime to grow strong enough to be able to take care of himself. Your little child is feebler than the tiger's cub, and you yourself are impotent before the lightning, the wind, the flame, the plague, and the wild beasts of the wilderness. Still more weak is man, morally and spiritually. His own nature is hopelessly broken down by the love and power of sin; his own tendencies are wrong; and spiritual forces of evil around him on every side tend to draw him away from the path of right and safety.

The salvation of the Lord Jesus Christ, therefore, comes to us with the promise of divine power, and the instrument of this power is the Holy Spirit.

A. B. Simpson
When the Comforter Came

HYMN FOR TODAY

Child of the kingdom, be filled with the Spirit.
Nothing but fullness thy longing can meet;
'Tis the enduement for life and for service—
Thine is the promise, so certain, so sweet.
"I will pour water on him who is thirsty,
I will pour floods upon the dry ground;
Open your heart for the gift I am bringing.
While ye are seeking me, I will be found."
> *"Ho, Everyone That Is Thirsty"—Lucy J. Rider*

FRUIT FOR TODAY

If this coming Sunday morning during your worship service a five-year-old boy marched himself right up the center aisle and boldly declared, "I want everyone out of this church in five minutes," I'm sure an usher would march up to the little guy and escort him down to children's church where he belonged. He wouldn't be much of a threat.

However, if a five-year-old boy marched himself right up the center aisle carrying a stick of dynamite and a lighter and declared the same command, the reaction would be dramatically different. Small boys with "hot air" are one thing, small boys with dynamite are another.

Jesus promised us power, you and me. This power is designed to enable us to speak and live the adventure we call the Christian life.

Today, don't underestimate yourself, especially as you are indwelt by the Holy Spirit. You are His witness. You are equipped through this extraordinary power! You are only one, but you are one, and you can make a "dynamite" difference in your world.

WEEK FOUR: Day Seven
Theme: Bondage Broken

SEED FOR TODAY

Then the LORD said to Moses, "Get up early in the morning, confront Pharaoh and say to him, 'This is what the LORD, the God of the Hebrews, says: Let my people go, so that they may worship me, or this time I will send the full force of my plagues against you and against your officials and your people, so you may know that there is no one like me in all the earth. . . .'" (Exodus 9:13-14)

LIGHT FOR TODAY

As God's people were held by Pharaoh in the bondage of Egypt, so God has His people in every known and unknown tribe of the earth, who are held in worse bondage than that of Egypt. God proposes in His plan of redemption to release a people for His name.

All human beings are God's creation and possession. Temporarily Satan has usurped authority, and through sin, holds the race in bondage. As God sent Moses to say over and over again to Pharaoh, "Let my people go!" so He has sent the Lord Jesus to save the world. He has commanded us to be His ministers to the last race of people in the uttermost parts of the earth, saying in the name of the Lord Jesus, the Creator and only Saviour, "Let my people go!"

Our work is not to try and improve the social conditions of the people of Egypt, but to call them out of Egypt, and into a new life. They become verily new creatures in Christ Jesus, living transformed lives, speaking a new language, the language of Zion, and singing a new song, "Worthy is the Lamb that was slain!"

Robert Jaffray
The Pioneer

HYMN FOR TODAY

Rescue the perishing,
Care for the dying,
Snatch them in pity from sin and the grave;

Weep o'er the erring one,
Lift up the fallen,
Tell them of Jesus the mighty to save.
Rescue the perishing,
Care for the dying;
Jesus is merciful,
Jesus will save.
"Rescue the Perishing"—Fanny J. Crosby

FRUIT FOR TODAY

Missionaries are men and women who carry the message to the unreached peoples of the world. The spirit of Moses resides in these precious instruments who shuttle the faith into the dark regions of our globe.

Today, pray for a missionary family—for boldness and open doors and bondage-breaking power.

Write a missionary family a short note expressing to them the earnest prayer you tendered to God in order that they might be bondage breakers like Moses.

Give a generous gift to a missionary family or missionary cause this month so that resources may be available for the "letting go of God's people" who reside in chains fashioned by the bondage of the world, the flesh and the devil.

WEEK FIVE: Day One
Theme: Mercy

SEED FOR TODAY

Remember, O LORD, your great mercy and love,
  for they are from of old.
Remember not the sins of my youth
  and my rebellious ways;
according to your love remember me,
  for you are good, O LORD. (Psalm 25:6-7)

LIGHT FOR TODAY

God blesses us because of His abundant mercy, the mercy which He bestowed upon us, and not because of any of our goodness. I do not believe that heaven itself will ever permit us to forget that we are recipients of the goodness of God and for that reason I do not believe that you and I will ever be permitted to forget Calvary.

Another thing in this regard is that although God wants His people to be holy as He is holy, He does not deal with us according to the degree of our holiness but according to the abundance of His mercy. Honesty requires us to admit this.

We do believe in justice and we do believe in judgment. We believe the only reason mercy triumphs over judgment is that God, by a divine, omniscient act of redemption, fixed it so man could escape justice and live in the sea of mercy. The justified man, the man who believes in Jesus Christ, born anew and now a redeemed child of God, lives in that mercy always.

The unjust man, however—the unrepentant sinner—lives in it now in a lesser degree, but the time will come when he will face the judgment of God. Though he had been kept by the mercy of God from death, from insanity, from disease, he can violate that mercy, turn his back on it and walk into judgment. Then it is too late!

A. W. Tozer
I Call It Heresy!

HYMN FOR TODAY

When this passing world is done,
When has sunk yon glaring sun,
When I stand with Christ in glory,
Looking o'er life's finished story
Then, Lord shall I fully know,
Not till then, how much I owe.
　　　"When This Passing World Is Done"
　　　—Robert M. McCheyne

FRUIT FOR TODAY

The technology of our time has permitted meteorologists to warn us of impending storms. The alarm is sounded in advance and proper precautions can be executed to spare the potential victims the terror of being unprepared for disaster. Our heavenly Father has not only warned us of impending catastrophe, He has provided us shelter from all that confronts us.

The Lord Jesus Christ aggressively dealt with our inability to protect ourselves from the harsh elements that would destroy us, not only in time but for eternity. He did not owe us this accommodation; we did not deserve His acts of sacrifice and love.

Mercy is the *modus operandi* of God the Father and God the Son. Today, reflect upon the words of Joseph Addison:

When all Thy mercies, O my God,
My rising soul surveys,
Transported with the view, I'm lost
In wonder love and praise!

Get lost in the mercy of God—because you truly have been found!

WEEK FIVE: Day Two
Theme: Christ in Me

SEED FOR TODAY

To them God has chosen to make known among the Gentiles the glorious riches of this mystery, which is Christ in you, the hope of glory. (Colossians 1:27)

LIGHT FOR TODAY

It is a glorious revelation that Christ will live in us and manifest Himself to us. Can we take in this sublime truth with its stupendous significance? The Christ who was born as a babe in Bethlehem; who grew to manhood in the humble home in Nazareth; who lived a life of holy obedience to His Father's will; who died on the cross as a sacrifice for sin; who ascended to heaven and seated Himself at the right hand of God as Advocate and High Priest; and who is coming back again to this dark and sin-cursed earth to transform it into Edenic beauty and reign in righteousness and peace; this blessed Christ of God will come into my poor heart and make His home there and live out His own life within me by the indwelling presence and power of the Holy Spirit. . . .

Far more sublime and glorious than either eradication or suppression is the truth of the indwelling Christ. Eradication would take out of the heart the principle of sin, while suppression would keep the principle of sin bound down and in subjection to the heart. But sanctification through the indwelling Christ means that not only the principle of sin, but the heart itself in which the principle of sin resides; yea more—the very person himself in his entire being is nailed to the cross and is raised again in vital union with the Lord. So that we may now say with Paul, "I have been crucified with Christ and I no longer live, but Christ lives in me. The life I live in the body, I live by faith in the Son of God, who loved me and gave himself for me" (Galatians 2:20).

George P. Pardington
The Crisis of the Deeper Life

HYMN FOR TODAY

This is my wonderful story—
Christ to my heart has come;
Jesus, the King of glory,
Finds in my heart a home.
Christ in me, Christ in me,
Christ in me—Oh, wonderful story;
Christ in me, Christ in me,
Christ in me, the hope of glory.
      "Christ in Me"—A. B. Simpson

FRUIT FOR TODAY

The Old Testament featured the *tabernacle*, a movable sanctuary in the wilderness. This "put up and take down" center of worship was replaced by the *temple*, a permanent dwelling which was immobile.

The New Testament features a significant paradigm shift as human beings are designated the depositories for the Holy Spirit given by Jesus Christ. This permits the worship, witness and work of God to be dispersed to every place where men and women exist. The focus shifts from buildings to bodies!

Today, if you are a Christian, you are the "temple" of the living God. You and I, as indwelt people, shuttle the message of salvation and sanctification wherever we go. The Church stands where you stand!

WEEK FIVE: Day Three
Theme: The Rut

SEED FOR TODAY

Therefore, if anyone is in Christ, he is a new creation; the old has gone, the new has come! . . . We are therefore Christ's ambassadors, as though God were making his appeal through us. We

implore you on Christ's behalf: Be reconciled to God. God made
him who had no sin to be sin for us, so that in him we might
become the righteousness of God. (2 Corinthians 5:17, 20-21)

LIGHT FOR TODAY

Why are people in the rut? There are several possibilities. They
may never have been truly converted at all, and this is one of our
great problems now. We have a dozen ways of getting people into
the kingdom of God, when the Lord said there was only one. They
leak in, ooze in, come in by osmosis and get in by marriage—just
get in by any kind of way. But there is only one true way. When
people find that after being in the church for years they are not
making much progress, they ought to examine themselves and
wonder whether they have truly been converted. True conversion
means radical repentance, a changed life, conscious forgiveness of
sin and a spiritual rebirth. Genuinely converted people, as the old
Methodists said, had a radical repentance, which eventuated in a
changed life. Then here came a consciousness of forgiveness of sins
and a spiritual rebirth. People in the rut may never have had that
at all.

A. W. Tozer
Rut, Rot or Revival

HYMN FOR TODAY

A ruler once came to Jesus by night
To ask Him the way of salvation and light;
The Master made answer in words true and plain,
"Ye must be born again."
"Ye must be born again,
Ye must be born again,
I verily, verily say unto you,
Ye must be born again."
    "Ye Must Be Born Again"—William T. Sleeper

FRUIT FOR TODAY

The "Half-way Covenant" (1662) was an attempt by reformers in New England to extend the jurisdiction of the church. The Massachusetts Synod asserted that baptized adults who lived uprightly, but who had no conversion experience could be accepted as church members. Their children were baptized as "halfway" members. Although this practice enlarged the cross-section of New Englanders who could join the church, it also weakened the fabric of the church and eroded its orthodoxy because it did not make conversion a prerequisite!

Every individual must encounter God in a personal experience. The Christian faith is not transferred or passed by osmosis, rather it is by metamorphosis that a person is confronted and converted by the Holy Spirit!

Today, if you have been changed by the living Christ through His Spirit, lift a word or song of praise toward Him! If you are tentative about your transformation, take time to invite God to do a work in your heart so that your name may be recorded in heaven's directory. "You must be born again!"

WEEK FIVE: Day Four
Theme: Discipleship

SEED FOR TODAY

"Suppose one of you wants to build a tower. Will he not first sit down and estimate the cost to see if he has enough money to complete it? For if he lays the foundation and is not able to finish it, everyone who sees it will ridicule him, saying, 'This fellow began to build and was not able to finish.' " (Luke 14:28-30)

LIGHT FOR TODAY

The church is a community of faith under construction. *Church*, from the Greek word *ekklesia*, means "the chosen band" or "called-out ones." The word *discipline* comes from the word *disciple* that describes someone who is both learning and being trained under the guidance of a master. In other words, a Christian is one who has become a disciple of Jesus Christ; the church is a school where discipleship is both learned and experienced.

When Jesus began his ministry, he chose twelve disciples who should be with him that they might be taught and trained to carry on the work he had begun. Later, during Christ's ministry, his popularity took a sharp upswing and great multitudes began to follow him (Luke 14:25). Jesus confronted the followers with the cost involved—it would involve family, friends, and life itself! . . .

A true disciple is to be willing to recognize what is involved and is prepared to accept the cost. A foundation is not enough. There is a goal to achieve in discipleship even after becoming disciples. Effective discipleship is neither a fad nor a blind step of ignorance; it is a new way of life to be given careful and deliberate calculation.

Samuel J. Stoesz
Church and Membership
Awareness

HYMN FOR TODAY

> *Take my life, and let it be*
> *Consecrated, Lord, to Thee.*
> *Take my moments and my days,*
> *Let them flow in ceaseless praise,*
> *Let them flow in ceaseless praise.*
> *Take my hands, and let them move*
> *At the impulse of Thy love.*
> *Take my feet, and let them be*
> *Swift and beautiful for Thee,*
> *Swift and beautiful for Thee.*
>> *"Take My Life, and Let It Be"—Francis R. Havergal*

FRUIT FOR TODAY

A picture's value is enhanced by what it contains in it, but it is also enhanced by what is left out of it! Discipleship involves setting priorities. The Christian cannot include every pursuit in his or her daily walk with Jesus Christ. As the Holy Spirit grants discernment, the disciple must narrow the focus of life, majoring on majors. This pruning of the plant is costly and results in "downsizing." However, the process leads to efficiency of service and enhanced production of fruit.

The early followers of the Wesleyan movement were nicknamed "Methodists" because they were methodical about the disciplines of their faith. They majored on such practices as Bible study, confession, prayer, and giving. They became so strong and lean in their faith that they shook the world! In a generic sense, we should all be "Methodists."

Today, omit something from the picture in order that your daily snapshot may be sharper, more clearly defined. Today, devote more time to primary pursuits of your life!

WEEK FIVE: Day Five
Theme: Praise

SEED FOR TODAY
I will praise you, O Lord my God, with all my heart;
  I will glorify your name forever. (Psalm 86:12)

LIGHT FOR TODAY
The average Christian life is woefully lacking in praise to God. The kind of testimony we hear from many is this: "We are doing the best we can to hold out in our poor weak way; pray for us that we may be faithful to the end." I've tried a few times to start a prayer meeting with a season of praise; and have asked people not to *ask* God for a thing, but to praise Him. I've never made it go but once. Every other time somebody slipped, and while one person would praise the Lord, and another would begin all right, it would not be

long before some one would say: "Then Lord, bless my children, give me—gi'me—gi'me—" they had to get that "Give me" in somewhere. Many are just "give me" Christians. This is about all the Lord hears from us; and it must be very disappointing to the angels, to see people who have been privileged as we are, living without constant praise in their hearts to God. Jesus cleansed ten lepers but only one returned to glorify God. It is an awful tragedy not to have a heart that is filled with praise, but to live on that low level where you are just simply trying to do the best you can.

Paul Rader
God's Blessed Man

HYMN FOR TODAY

Praise Him! Praise Him! Jesus our blessed Redeemer!
Sing, O earth; His wonderful love proclaim!
Hail Him! Hail Him! Highest archangels in glory;
Strength and honor give to His holy name!
Like a shepherd Jesus will guard His children;
In His arms He carries them all day long.
Praise Him! Praise Him! Tell of His excellent greatness;
Praise Him! Praise Him, ever in joyful song!
"Praise Him! Praise Him!"—Fanny Crosby

FRUIT FOR TODAY

The Northeast region of the United States and most of the Southeast experienced the "Storm of the Century" on March 13, 1993. In central Pennsylvania we received 24 inches of snow. This record snowfall was blown about by gale winds which created drifts as high as 10 feet! The next day on Sunday morning six people showed up for church. Two people arrived on skis and two made their journey in a snowmobile.

I recall making my way to church soon after the fury of the storm had passed. I was sensitive to the singing of the birds; their songs were filled with merriment and expressed bold vitality. Despite the storm they uttered a song.

The old gospel song poses this challenge: "Anyone can sing when the sun's shining bright, but you need a song in the night."

Today, sing! Make melody in your heart! Someone in the storm may hear you and take courage!

WEEK FIVE: Day Six
Theme: In His Steps

SEED FOR TODAY
To this you were called, because Christ suffered for you, leaving you an example, that you should follow in his steps. (1 Peter 2:21)

LIGHT FOR TODAY
The character and life of Christ have a completeness of detail which no other Bible biography possesses. The story has been written out by many witnesses, and the portrait is reproduced in all its lineaments and features. He has traversed every stage of life from the cradle to the grave, and represented humanity in every condition and circumstance of temptation, trial and need, so that His example is equally suited to childhood, youth or manhood. It is suited to the humble and poor in life's lowliest path or to the sovereign who sways the widest scepter, for Jesus is at once the lowly Nazarene and the Lord of lords.

Christ has felt the throb of every human affection. He has felt the pang of every human sorrow. He is the Son of Man in the largest, broadest sense. Nay, His humanity is so complete that He represents the softer traits of womanhood as well as the virility and strength of manhood and even the simplicity of a little child. There is no place in the experiences of life where we may not look back at this Pattern Life for light and help as we bring it into touch with our need and ask, "What would Jesus do?"

> A. B. Simpson
> *The Fourfold Gospel*

HYMN FOR TODAY

'Tis better far to follow Jesus,
No matter where His hand may lead,
Than with the world's vain fleeting pleasures
Our souls' immortal longings feed;
For He has made us for His glory
And His are joys that never die;
'Tis sweeter far to follow Jesus,
For He alone can satisfy.

" *'Tis Better Far to Follow Jesus"—May A. Stephens*

FRUIT FOR TODAY

What is the guiding or defining principle of your life?

Charles Sheldon wrote *In His Steps*, the fictional story of a minister named Henry Maxwell who challenged his congregation to live life for one year by this question, "What would Jesus do?"

Many who accepted this thesis found their lives revolutionized by this new approach to living. The editor of the local newspaper used his influence to create a vehicle for morality via the printed page. The college president used his education to improve the city's ethical health and to address the needs of the poor and oppressed. A businessman became a mentor for hundreds of young men who would establish their own companies. Marriages were entered into and engagements broken based upon the principles which emerged in the life of Jesus!

Today, when you come to a fork in the road, a tight ethical corner, a tough moral decision, ask the question, "What would Jesus do?" When you follow Jesus you will discover the higher road!

Our Lord stated it boldly: "I am the way" (John 14:6). Don't get sidetracked! Look for His footprints and you will be a person "in the way."

WEEK FIVE: Day Seven
Theme: The Cost of Discipleship

SEED FOR TODAY

Then he called the crowd to him along with his disciples and said: "If anyone would come after me, he must deny himself and take up his cross and follow me. For whoever wants to save his life will lose it, but whoever loses his life for me and for the gospel will save it. (Mark 8:34-35)

LIGHT FOR TODAY

Things have become necessary to us, a development never originally intended. God's gifts now take the place of God, and the whole course of nature is upset by the monstrous substitution.

Our Lord referred to this tyranny of things when He said to His disciples, "If any man will come after me, let him deny himself, and take up his cross, and follow me. For whosoever will save his life shall lose it: and whosoever shall lose his life for my sake shall find it."

Breaking this truth into fragments for our better understanding, it would seem that there is within each of us an enemy which we tolerate at our peril. Jesus called it "life" and "self," or as we would say, the self-life. Its chief characteristic is its possessiveness: the words "gain" and "profit" suggest this. To allow this enemy to live is in the end to lose everything. To repudiate it and give up all for Christ is to lose nothing at last, but to preserve everything unto life eternal. And possibly also a hint is given here as to the only effective way to destroy this foe: it is by the Cross. "Let him take up his cross and follow me."

A. W. Tozer
The Pursuit of God

HYMN FOR TODAY

My Jesus, I love Thee, I know Thou art mine,
For Thee all the follies of sin I resign;
My gracious Redeemer, my Saviour art Thou,

If ever I loved Thee, my Jesus, 'tis now.
  "My Jesus, I Love Thee"—William R. Featherstone

FRUIT FOR TODAY

Jim Elliot was a missionary to the Auca Indians in Peru. He was martyred in one of the most publicized accounts of missionary sacrifice documented in the 20th century. It was Elliot who articulated the classic Christian motto: "He is no fool who gives what he cannot keep, to gain what he cannot lose."

It is tempting in our time to buy into the consumer mentality. We practice the "Gospel of Get" rather than the "Gospel of Give." What have you given up or lost recently that nudged you closer to God?

Today, deny yourself of one issue or item for the glory of God! You'll never keep up with Jesus if you carry too much luggage.

WEEK SIX: Day One
Theme: Baptism

SEED FOR TODAY

Or don't you know that all of us who were baptized into Christ Jesus were baptized into his death? We were therefore buried with him through baptism into death in order that, just as Christ was raised from the dead through the glory of the Father, we too may live a new life. (Romans 6:3-4)

LIGHT FOR TODAY

Of this two-fold identification of the believer with Christ in His death and resurrection baptism is an impressive symbolical representation. The popular conception of the ordinance of baptism is that it is a sort of badge of Christianity. Just as a member of a lodge or fraternal order receives a badge or medal as evidence of his initiation, so baptism is regarded as a sign of membership in a Christian church. There is of course a measure of truth in this view, inasmuch as baptism is one of the marks of distinction between a believer and an unbeliever. But Christian baptism is the sign and seal of our *union* with Christ, and the Lord's Supper is a sign and seal of our *communion* with Christ.

Baptism has a two-fold significance. In the first place, it is the outward sign and visible seal of the inner work of grace wrought by the Spirit of God in regeneration. It is the testimony before the world of the fact of conversion. It is a personal confession of Jesus Christ as Savior and Lord and of the decision to follow His footsteps in holy obedience. . . .

But, in the second place, baptism in its deeper spiritual meaning is a symbol of death. It is not a rite of cleansing, but a type of crucifixion. . . .

Thus, baptism is a symbolical representation of the believer's death, burial and resurrection with Christ. It is, as someone has graphically expressed it, "the funeral service of the old life."

On the one hand, we are "buried with him through baptism into death" and on the other hand we are "raised with Him through your faith in the power of God," in order that "just as Christ was raised from the dead through the glory of the Father, we too live a new life."

George P. Pardington
The Crisis of the Deeper Life

HYMN FOR TODAY

> *Buried in baptism with our Lord,*
> *We rise with Him to life restored.*
> *Not the bare life in Adam lost—*
> *One richer far, for more it cost.*
> *"Buried in Baptism with Our Lord"—Anonymous*

FRUIT FOR TODAY

The classic description of baptism is "an outward sign of an inward work of grace." One candidate in a membership class contributed this definition, "an outward profession of an inward possession." The classic and the contemporary definitions are both beneficial to the understanding of this event.

Have you been baptized? Jesus was! If He is normative for the Christian faith then every believer should pursue this sacrament. Jesus, Peter and Paul commanded baptism in the New Testament. The Great Commission incorporates baptism into the objectives of the disciples: ". . . baptizing them in the name of the Father and of the Son and of the Holy Spirit" (Matthew 28:19).

Today, commit yourself to this act of obedience. If you have complied, commit to giving proof of the resurrection life you possess in Jesus Christ. Your inward possession should be showing!

WEEK SIX: Day Two
Theme: Fasting

SEED FOR TODAY

There was also a prophetess, Anna, the daughter of Phanuel, of the tribe of Asher. She was very old; she had lived with her husband seven years after her marriage, and then was a widow until she was eighty-four. She never left the temple but worshiped night and day, fasting and praying. (Luke 2:36-37)

LIGHT FOR TODAY

Fasting is not so much for God as it is for the person who is praying. The withdrawal from satisfying the desires of the body seems to strengthen the inner human spirit. It makes the person more sensitive to God, sin and demonic powers. It increases faith and spiritual boldness. It gives him heightened insight into his own problems or those of others. The will and guidance of God becomes more clear. The withdrawal from physical desire makes his personal health seem less important than the glory of God. Fasting has an inner purifying effect that makes the one who is fasting and praying a cleaner channel for the will and working of God. . . . If you sense that God is leading you to fast and pray about your problem, you would be wise to study carefully what the Bible has to say on this subject. I advise you also to seek counsel from some godly person who practices fasting. Then proceed under God's direction.

Richard Sipley
Understanding Divine Healing

HYMN FOR TODAY

Take time to be holy—
Speak oft with thy Lord;
Abide in Him always,
And feed on His Word.
Make friends of God's children;
Help those who are weak,

Forgetting in nothing
His blessing to seek.

Take time to be holy—
Be calm in thy soul,
Each thought and each motive
Beneath His control.
Thus, led by His Spirit,
To fountains of love,
Thou soon shalt be fitted
For service above.
> *"Take Time to Be Holy"*
> *—William D. Longstaff*

FRUIT FOR TODAY

Fasting is abstaining from physical food in order to feed upon prayer and the Word of God. Jesus allotted time for fasting (Matthew 4:2). The early church employed fasting in the process of selecting and commissioning missionaries and elders (Acts 13:2; 14:23). The Pharisees found a way to pervert this sacrificial discipline by looking downcast and by disfiguring their appearance so that people would applaud their religious devotion (Matthew 6:16).

Today, carve out one meal in your schedule during the week when you will substitute additional spiritual nourishment for physical food. Factor in a time of fasting, unheralded and unannounced to family and friends. The meal which the heavenly Father provides may surprise you and delight you!

WEEK SIX: Day Three
Theme: Prayer

SEED FOR TODAY

Now to him who is able to do immeasurably more than all we ask or imagine, according to his power that is at work within us, to him be glory in the church and in Christ Jesus throughout all generations, for ever and ever! Amen. (Ephesians 3:20-21)

LIGHT FOR TODAY

The victories of prayer are the mountaintops of the Bible. They take us back to the plains of Mamre, to the fords of Peniel, to the prison of Joseph, to the triumphs of Moses, to the victories of Joshua, to the deliverances of David and to the miracles of Elijah and Elisha. The victories of prayer take us back to the whole story of the Master's life, to the secret of Pentecost, to the keynote of Paul's unparalleled ministry, to the lives of the saints and the deaths of martyrs, and to all that is most sacred and sweet in the history of the church and the experience of God's children.

Some day the last conflict will have passed, and the footstool of prayer will have given place to the harp of praise. The scenes of earth that will be gilded most with eternal radiance will be those often linked with sorrow and darkest night. Then, over it all we may read the inscription: "Jehovah Shamma—the Lord was there"! Only that which God touched shall be remembered or be worth remembering forever. These will be imperishable memorials. From this day forward may they cover every pathway and every step of life's journey! And may we recognize that whatever comes is but another call to prayer and another opportunity for God to manifest His glory and to erect an everlasting memorial of His victorious love!

A. B. Simpson
The Life of Prayer

HYMN FOR TODAY

What a friend we have in Jesus,
All our sins and griefs to bear!
What a privilege to carry
Everything to God in prayer!
Oh, what peace we often forfeit,

Oh, what needless pain we bear,
All because we do not carry
Everything to God in prayer!
     "What a Friend We Have in Jesus"
     —Joseph M. Scriven

FRUIT FOR TODAY

Above the entryway leading from the living room to the kitchen in our home in Shippensburg, Pennsylvania, was a plaque which asked this question, "Have you prayed about it?" If God is who He claims to be, and prayer can do what the Bible claims it can do, then the answer should be a resounding "Yes!" Prayer should be the knee-jerk response of the Christian. Prayer should be the first plan of action, not a leftover alternative.

Today, as you confront your inconveniences, your opponents, your delays, as you stand before closed doors that must be open, you have this incredible access to the Almighty God. The angel delivered Mary this open-ended promise, "For nothing is impossible with God" (Luke 1:37). Later, Mary was commended by Elizabeth for her response to the angel's stunning declaration that she would experience a virgin birth, "Blessed is she who has believed what the Lord has said to her will be accomplished!" (1:45). *Have you prayed about it?*

WEEK SIX: *Day Four*
Theme: Giving

SEED FOR TODAY

But just as you excel in everything—in faith, in speech, in knowledge, in complete earnestness and in your love for us—see that you also excel in this grace of giving. (2 Corinthians 8:7)

LIGHT FOR TODAY

What is grace? Grace is something given us, something we get, not something we give. God does not require us to give as though it was a difficult exercise. He wants to give us the spirit of giving. Giving is something we must do in the power of the Holy Spirit. It is something we must take as a divine gift, a grace of the Holy Spirit. Therefore giving belongs to the essential qualities of holiness and right living. Without this grace we cannot call ourselves truly sanctified children of God. Thankfully, because it is a grace, it is available to each of us.

Giving is a privilege of the poor. The very poorest may give and God will enable them to give. Giving is not for the wealthy, for the millionaire. It is for the humble and the poor, for those of the smallest resources and the most modest means. It was "in a great trial of affliction" and out of "deep poverty" that the Macedonians gave. . . . It is God's doing, not man's. Therefore God chooses the weakest of the people to do it. . . .

Grace is what God can do, not what we can do. Give, believing that God can supply even more than you can see of resources and ability. Believe that He can save for you and enable you to do in this as in other things more than you could in yourself—even beyond your power.

A. B. Simpson
Missionary Messages

HYMN FOR TODAY

Give of thy sons to bear the message glorious;
Give of thy wealth to speed them on their way;
Pour out thy soul for them in prayer victorious;
And all thou spendest Jesus will repay.
Publish glad tidings,
Tidings of peace,
Tidings of Jesus, redemption and release.
"O Zion, Haste"—Mary A. Thomson

FRUIT FOR TODAY

Don't underestimate the power of your pocketbook in God's work! When resources are slim because people misappropriate their funds this has a suffocating effect on vital ministries. When believers participate in "grace giving," that is, spirit-led stewardship, the church moves forward with great strides.

The utilization of money is a significant barometer of spiritual growth in the individual's life and a formidable factor in determining the level of spiritual conquest in a church, district or denomination.

Today, is it time for you to take a step forward in the grace of giving? The next time you prepare your offering envelope, pause to petition the Lord to enable you to give with grace! This exercise—which at first seemed so routine—may give you unexpected joy and pleasure.

WEEK SIX: Day Five
Theme: Listening to God

SEED FOR TODAY
Be still, and know that I am God;
  I will be exalted among the nations,
  I will be exalted in the earth. (Psalm 46:10)

LIGHT FOR TODAY

Whoever will listen will hear the speaking heaven. This is definitely not the hour when men take kindly to an exhortation to listen, for listening is not today a part of popular religion. We are at the opposite end of the pole from there. Religion has accepted the monstrous heresy that noise, size, activity and bluster make a man dear to God. But we may take heart. To a people caught in the still of the tempest of the last great conflict God says, "Be still, and know that I am God," and still He says it, as if He means to tell us that our strength and safety lie not in noise but in silence.

It is important that we get still to wait on God. And it is best that we get alone, preferably with our Bible outspread before us. Then if we will we may draw near to God and begin to hear Him speak to us in our hearts. I think for the average person the progression will be something like this: First a sound as of a Presence walking in the garden. Then a voice, more intelligible but still far from clear. Then the happy moment when the Spirit begins to illuminate the Scriptures, and that which has only been a sound, or at best a voice, now becomes an intelligible word, warm and intimate and clear as the word of a dear friend. Then will come life and light, and best of all, ability to see and rest in and embrace Jesus Christ as Saviour and Lord and All.

A.W. Tozer
The Pursuit of God

HYMN FOR TODAY

There is a place of quiet rest
Near to the heart of God,
A place where sin cannot molest,
Near to the heart of God.
O Jesus, blest Redeemer,
Sent from the heart of God,
Hold us, who wait before Thee,
Near to the heart of God.
"Near to the Heart of God"—Cleland B. McAfee

FRUIT FOR TODAY

The expression, "Silence is golden," has merit for the devotional life of the Christian. The average person in today's frantic world is accustomed to and even addicted to noise. Appliances such as radio and television can inundate the world with sound and data. People take walks with a *Walkman®*, an apparatus that insures that the incessant sounds of our culture will continue to invade our moments of quietness and reflection. It is a rare individual who can put the noise on the shelf and open a channel to God!

There is a beauty and splendor in tranquility. There is value in listening to the manifestations of natural theology such as a rippling brook or a robin's solo. There is spiritual precedent in permitting God to talk during our daily exercise of personal prayer, which is to be a dialogue, not a monologue.

Today, decrease the decibels so that you may increase the reception and retention of the heavenly Voice. You may hear something which will change your "walk" in this world. Don't underestimate the potential of silence and stillness.

WEEK SIX: Day Six
Theme: Using God

SEED FOR TODAY
But seek first his kingdom and his righteousness, and all these things will be given to you as well. (Matthew 6:33)

LIGHT FOR TODAY
I feel that we must repudiate this great, modern wave of seeking God for His benefits. The sovereign God wants to be loved for Himself and honored for Himself, but that is only part of what He wants. The other part is that He wants us to know that when we have Him, we have everything—we have all the rest. Jesus made that plain when He said, "Seek ye first the kingdom of God and His righteousness, and all these things shall be added unto you."

It seems that Christian believers have been going through a process of indoctrination and brainwashing, so that it has become easy for us to adopt a kind of creed that makes God to be our servant instead of our being God's servant. . . .

John Wesley believed that men ought to seek God alone because God is love, and he advised people in his day: "If anyone comes preaching and tells you to seek anything more than love, do not listen, do not listen!" I think in our day we are in need of such an admonition as, "Seek more of God—and seek Him for Himself alone!" If we became serious-minded about this, we would soon discover that all of the gifts of God come along with the knowledge and the presence of God Himself.

A. W. Tozer
I Talk Back to the Devil

HYMN FOR TODAY

O Love that gave itself for me,
Help me to love and live like Thee,
And kindle in this heart of mine
The passion fire of love divine.
O Love divine,
O Love divine,
Revive this longing heart of mine,
And kindle in me from above
The living fire of heavenly love.
    "O Love Divine"—A. B. Simpson

FRUIT FOR TODAY

Marvin Hinton wrote a book on prayer with the title, *God Is Not a Vending Machine*. The Christian should not approach God as a consumer looking for the best bargains that yield liberal returns. Rather, the Sermon on the Mount recommends that we seek God's kingdom and righteousness first—then other dividends will follow!

Loving God and complying with His commandments bring their own rewards! The actualization of our lives, our self-fulfillment, is found in worshiping God and serving in His eternal enterprise.

Today, ask not what God can do for you—ask what you can do for Him!

WEEK SIX: Day Seven
Theme: A Right View of Sin

SEED FOR TODAY

But now that you have been set free from sin and have become slaves to God, the benefit you reap leads to holiness, and the result is eternal life. For the wages of sin is death, but the gift of God is eternal life in Christ Jesus our Lord. (Romans 6:22-23)

LIGHT FOR TODAY

There is one great reason for denying the reality of sin. It is a wish to apologize for it and indulge in it. There are those that argue that it is a kind of fate or destiny, the result of circumstances for which men are not responsible. Or, they argue, it is only reality to *us*; it is only *our* view of things; the great and infinite God cannot be concerned with it. He looks down upon us with pity, indulgence and compassion. It cannot matter to Him what we do; we cannot touch His majesty or His holiness. So men apologize for sin instead of trying to escape from it. They deny its reality in order to plunge into it. They find in their reasoning a method of saving themselves not *from* sin, but *in* sin. . . .

Man calls sin an accident; God calls it an abomination. Man calls it a blunder; God calls it a blindness. Man calls it a chance; God calls it a choice. Man calls it a defect; God calls it a disease. Man calls it an error; God calls it a fatality. Man calls it an heredity; God calls it a habit. Man calls it an incident; God calls it an inclination. Man calls it an infirmity; God calls it an iniquity. Man calls it a luxury; God calls it a leprosy. Man calls it a liberty; God calls it a lawlessness. Man calls it a mistake; God calls it a madness. Man calls it a peccadillo; God calls it a poison. Man calls it a relapse; God calls it a rebellion. Man calls it a slip; God calls it a suicide. Man calls it a trifle; God calls it a tragedy. Man calls it a thoughtlessness; God calls it a thraldom [slavery]. Man calls it a weakness; God calls it a wickedness.

J. Gregory Mantle
The Counterfeit Christ

HYMN FOR TODAY

I hear Thy welcome voice
That calls me, Lord, to Thee
For cleansing in Thy precious blood
That flowed on Calvary.
I am coming, Lord,
Coming now to Thee!
Wash me, cleanse me in the blood
That flowed from Calvary.
    "I Am Coming, Lord"—Lewis Hartsough

FRUIT FOR TODAY

Karl Menninger's classic book, *Whatever Became of Sin*, contends that our culture has renamed sin, rewrapped sin; in essence, we have discovered ways to make sin more acceptable and less reprehensible. The society of the late twentieth century is upgrading a number of sins and creating a climate of social tolerance for them. Adultery, homosexuality and abortion have become legitimate manifestations of the human will and spirit.

God hates sin! God keeps records! And there is a day on which we will give account of ourselves to Him (Romans 14:12).

It is unfair to say that sin does not pay because it does. "The wages of sin is death" (Romans 6:23). It is inaccurate to say that sin is devoid of pleasure for the Bible acknowledges that there is pleasure in sin for a season (Hebrews 11:25). Seasons are transient, however, and the smart investor seeks dividends over the long haul.

Today, our compassionate heavenly Father promises this redemptive response, "If we confess our sins, he is faithful and just and will forgive us our sins and purify us from all unrighteousness" (1 John 1:9). Do you have any laundry to be done?

WEEK SEVEN: Day One
Theme: Resurrection

SEED FOR TODAY

Since, then, you have been raised with Christ, set your hearts on things above, where Christ is seated at the right hand of God. Set your minds on things above, not on earthly things. For you died, and your life is now hidden with Christ in God. (Colossians 3:1-3)

LIGHT FOR TODAY

The great objection to the teachings of natural religion and human ethics is that we are taught to rise to higher planes. The glory of the gospel is that it does not teach us to rise, but it shows our inability to do anything good of ourselves. It lays us at once in the grave in utter helplessness and nothingness, and then raises us up into a new life that is born from above and sustained by heavenly sources.

The Christian life is not something man initiates and maintains on his own; it is wholly supernatural and divine. The resurrection cannot come until there has been death. This is presupposed. The degree to which a person has died to self determines the measure of the resurrection life and power. Let us not fear, therefore, to die to self completely. We lose nothing by letting go, and we cannot enter in until we come out. If we are willing to be dead with Him, we shall also live with Him.

Colossians 3:1 expresses this idea: "Since, then, you have been raised with Christ, set your hearts on things above, where Christ is seated at the right hand of God." Paul did not tell the Colossians to die with Christ and rise with Him. Rather he calls upon Christians to take their places as having already died and risen.

A. B. Simpson

The Self-Life and the Christ-Life

HYMN FOR TODAY

Long my imprisoned spirit lay
Fastbound in sin and nature's night;
Thine eye diffused a quickening ray.
I woke, the dungeon flamed with light;
My chains fell off, my heart was free;
I rose, went forth, and followed Thee.
Amazing love! How can it be
That Thou, my God, shouldst die for me!
      "And Can It Be That I Should Gain"—Charles Wesley

FRUIT FOR TODAY

"How To" books have become one of the most successful genres of modern literature. Their "salability" testifies to humanity's desire to step up to the next level. A diet, an exercise program, a mnemonic technique—these may be the "missing link" to new appearance, health or vocational success.

The Christian, however, depends upon resources which are stationed outside the realm of human ingenuity and effort. There is an *otherness* about this faith in Jesus Christ which transports His disciples to the plane of the miraculous.

Today, reflect upon this premise: *you will never be able to fully explain all that God through Christ has done in and through you.* Expect the unexplainable because of the resurrection power which flows through the veins of your soul! The exhibition of a product which is not explainable by empirical evidence is one of God's most effective marketing strategies. *You verify the product!*

WEEK SEVEN: Day Two
Theme: Evangelism

SEED FOR TODAY

When I came to you, brothers, I did not come with eloquence or superior wisdom as I proclaimed to you the testimony about God. For I resolved to know nothing while I was with you except Jesus Christ and him crucified. I came to you in weakness and fear, and with much trembling. My message and my preaching were not with wise and persuasive words, but with a demonstration of the Spirit's power, so that your faith might not rest on men's wisdom, but on God's power. (1 Corinthians 2:1-5)

LIGHT FOR TODAY

The flaw in current evangelism lies in its humanistic approach. It struggles to be supernaturalistic but never quite makes it. It is frankly fascinated by the great, noisy, aggressive world with its big names, its hero worship, its wealth and garish pageantry. To the millions of disappointed persons who have always yearned for worldly glory but never attained it, the modern evangel offers a quick and easy short cut to their heart's desire. Peace of mind, happiness, prosperity, social acceptance, publicity, success in sports, business, the entertainment field, and perchance to sit occasionally at the same banquet table with a celebrity—all this on earth and heaven at last. Certainly no insurance company can offer half as much.

In this quasi-Christian scheme of things God becomes the Aladdin lamp who does the bidding of everyone that will accept His Son and sign a card. The total obligation of the sinner is discharged when he accepts Christ. After that he has but to come with his basket and receive the religious equivalent of everything the world offers and enjoy it to the limit. Those who have not accepted Christ must be content with this world, but the Christian gets this one with the one to come thrown in as a bonus. . . .

This concept of Christianity is in radical error, and because it touches the souls of men it is dangerous, even deadly, error. At the bottom it is little more than weak humanism allied with weak Christianity to give it ecclesiastical respectability. It may be identified by its religious approach. Invariably it begins with man and his needs and then looks around for God; true Christianity reveals God as searching for man to deliver him from his ambitions.

A. W. Tozer
Born After Midnight

HYMN FOR TODAY

Would you be free from the burden of sin?
There's power in the blood, power in the blood;
Would you o'er evil a victory win?
There's wonderful power in the blood.
There is power, power,
Wonderworking power
In the blood of the Lamb;
There is power, power,
Wonderworking power
In the precious blood of the Lamb.
      "There Is Power in the Blood"—Lewis E. Jones

FRUIT FOR TODAY

The essential ingredient in evangelism is the Holy Spirit. Methods may package it better or worse, messengers may serve it up in different ways, but evangelism is primarily a spiritual process. The term prevenient grace means "before-the-moment grace." Our God is the Author and Finisher of our faith through Jesus Christ and the Holy Spirit. It is imperative that we view evangelism as transcending what we can do with human resources. The indispensable ingredient is the work of the Spirit.

Today, don't put your hopes in messengers or methods, put your hopes in the Spirit of the Living God! Our weapons are not the weapons of the world. Do the best you can to pray for others and share your witness with others, but remember that it is only God who can administer the "new birth" needed to usher a man or woman into His eternal kingdom.

WEEK SEVEN: Day Three
Theme: Lordship

SEED FOR TODAY

I have been crucified with Christ and I no longer live, but Christ lives in me. The life I live in the body, I live by faith in the Son of God, who loved me and gave himself for me. (Galatians 2:20)

LIGHT FOR TODAY

Many of God's dear people have by faith received the fullness of the Holy Spirit but they still find themselves being impatient, especially in the home.

Many become irritated when they are falsely accused or slandered. They give way to sensitiveness or self-pity.

They begin to wonder: "Why should I have all these difficulties? Didn't I receive the fullness of the Holy Spirit as an act of faith after all?" . . .

Beloved, it is right here that many of us make our mistake. The truth is that the Holy Spirit does not make us humanly perfect and does not guarantee that we will automatically spend the rest of our lives on a spiritual mountaintop!

I think that many Christians honestly do not realize that the Spirit of God wants to show them their own self-life as God sees it. There cannot be full spiritual victory within any individual who is not willing to deal with that ugly life of self, applying God's own prescription of complete identification with the death of Jesus Christ. . . .

The only way that we can know His victory and His glory is just to let Him come in His fullness and take over. If we do not acknowledge this secret as the means of dealing with sin and self, we will never experience the gracious fulfillment of our being made one with Him, fused in our nature in oneness with the divine nature of our victor, Jesus Christ.

> R. Mabel Francis
> *Filled with the Spirit . . . Then What?*

HYMN FOR TODAY

> *I am trusting Thee, Lord Jesus,*
> *Trusting only Thee!*
> *Trusting Thee for full salvation,*
> *Great and free.*
> *I am trusting Thee for power;*
> *Thine can never fail;*
> *Words which Thou Thyself shalt give me*
> *Must prevail.*
> *"I Am Trusting Thee, Lord Jesus"—Francis Havergal*

FRUIT FOR TODAY

Who is driving the car? When a person accepts Jesus Christ into their life it is analogous to driving a car. He is invited to be a passenger in our vehicle but we are still behind the wheel. The Spirit-filled life understands there must be a change of driver and passenger. Jesus must be invited to sit in the *driver's* seat and the driver must slide over to the *passenger's* seat! The Lordship of Jesus Christ, with all its dividends, can only be realized if He controls the steering wheel.

Today, ask yourself this question: *Who is driving the car?* If Jesus is driving, you are in for quite a ride! If He is not, you may be traveling in circles. Allow Him to take the wheel—He is one incredible chauffeur!

WEEK SEVEN: Day Four
Theme: Christian Joy

SEED FOR TODAY

Be joyful always; pray continually; give thanks in all circumstances, for this is God's will for you in Christ Jesus. (1 Thessalonians 5:16-18)

LIGHT FOR TODAY

My life is far from a perpetual succession of crises.

Observers from the ranks of the uncommitted have often accused us Christians of morbidity. We sing about the burdens of life. We pray about our rheumatism, our arthritis, and our impending surgeries. Too often the sermon that moves us most is the one describing the valley rather than the mountaintop.

Surely God never intended the Christian adventure to be so characterized.

Nehemiah the prophet declared, "The joy of the Lord is your strength," and Jesus said, "These things have I spoken unto you, that my joy might remain in you, and that your joy might be full." Now I realize that even though the test of our joy comes when inclement circumstances disrupt the normal trend of life, these are but occasionals. The day-by-day mood of the Christian should be one of genuine exuberance, a tone of voice and a hue of countenance that are not mere facade but erupt from the reservoir of spiritual maturity.

Stanley Tam
God Owns My Business

HYMN FOR TODAY

The joy of the Lord is the strength of His people,
The sunshine that banishes sadness and gloom;
The fountain that bursts in the desert of sorrow,
And sheds o'er the wilderness gladness and bloom.
Oh, the joy of the Lord is our strength and our song;
Our sorrow and sighing are o'er;
We'll rejoice in the Lord,
We'll rejoice in the Lord,
We'll rejoice in the Lord evermore.
"The Joy of the Lord"—A. B. Simpson

FRUIT FOR TODAY

E. Stanley Jones reported in *Abundant Living* that a college girl, testifying about her conversion, said "I felt that I had swallowed sunshine." Joy is a trademark of triumphant Christianity. Our prayer meetings are often organ recitals rather than praise recitals. In *The Self-Life and the Christ-Life*, A.B. Simpson wrote:

> Our faith should be as bright as spring's new blossoms, as lively as the songs of the birds. Just as Jesus met the women on that bright resurrection morning with the message, "Greetings!" (Matthew 28:9), so He would greet us on the morning of our new life bidding us go forth with the joy of our Lord as our strength.

Today, if the world at large could read your countenance, what would be the "weather report"—sunny and pleasant, or stormy and threatening? Matthew 5:16 suggests this forecast: "In the same way, let your light shine before men, that they may see your good deeds and praise your Father in heaven."

WEEK SEVEN: Day Five
Theme: Discernment

SEED FOR TODAY
But when he, the Spirit of truth, comes, he will guide you into all truth. He will not speak on his own; he will speak only what he hears, and he will tell you what is yet to come. He will bring glory to me by taking from what is mine and making it known to you. (John 16:13-14)

LIGHT FOR TODAY
It is [the Holy Spirit's] clear goal to lead Christian believers in "all truth" (John 16:13).

That being so, it is also clear that the Holy Spirit is in the business of giving wisdom and discernment to Christians. I have seen cases where the Holy Spirit has given biblical references or scriptural texts to persons in need of help. I have seen a demon-possessed person in desperation call out scriptural references unknown to her. One of the Christian workers would simply read the text, and a demon would be expelled by the reading of the text alone.

Preachers often have the experience of receiving additional insight and flow of material in the warmth and glow of biblical preaching. Some of this may be human enthusiasm alone, but most often, I believe, the Holy Spirit brings the extra dimension.

Who can doubt then that the Holy Spirit brings discernment? He needs to be recognized. Appreciated. Respected. He must not be grieved or quenched. He wants to fill and control the Christian. He wants to exercise the spiritual gifts through the believers. He wants to adore and exalt Jesus Christ. But He is the Spirit who searcheth the hearts, who knows all things. Because He is a Spirit, He communicates with the human spirit.

The ancients got "yes" and "no" answers from God. Since they did not possess a complete Bible, more direct means of consultation were used. A prophet interceded and received discernment and guidance by direct revelation.

In the New Testament age believers have the Word and direct access by prayer. In this day, some suggest, the inner witness from the Holy Spirit may be negative or positive according to God's will. In any case both Paul and John talked about the inner witness. And it is true, the Holy Spirit communicates directly to the human spirit.

K. Neill Foster
The Discerning Christian

HYMN FOR TODAY

Open my eyes that I may see
Glimpses of truth Thou hast for me;
Place in my hands the wonderful key
That shall unclasp and set me free.
Silently now I wait for Thee,

Ready, my God, Thy will to see;
Open my eyes, illumine me,
Spirit divine!
   "Open My Eyes That I May See"—Clara H. Scott

FRUIT FOR TODAY

The Christian can employ multiple means to discern truth. The Holy Spirit is an experienced guide (John 16:13), and if the believer is "under His influence" there will be manifestations of illumination!

There are members of the body of Christ who possess the gift of discernment, who can decipher right from wrong with uncanny accuracy. These individuals are capable of "distinguishing between spirits" (1 Corinthians 12:10) and they should be accessed if we are unsure of another's motivation. Proverbs 24:6 advises that "for waging war you need guidance, and for victory many advisers."

There is collective discernment which is obtainable in the company of other brothers and sisters in Jesus Christ. A final and decisive factor is the Word of God. The Word is a lamp and light (Psalm 119:105).

Today, capitalize on the plurality of resources that are within your access so that your choices may be assets and not liabilities.

WEEK SEVEN: Day Six
Theme: Healing

SEED FOR TODAY

But for you who revere my name, the sun of righteousness will rise with healing in its wings. And you will go out and leap like calves released from the stall. (Malachi 4:2)

LIGHT FOR TODAY

The healing of the body through Jesus Christ was no new thought to the ancient prophets. It had been included in the covenant of Moses. It had been the theme of David's songs and Solomon's proverbs. It had been part of the simple practical faith that took God as their theocratic king for all the life of the nation. It had been a prime feature in the glorious picture which Isaiah gave of the Man of Sorrows. . . .

God always meant the faith of His people to take real things from Him and make eternal blessings stepping stones to the higher experiences of the unseen. For if God had not become real to us in the things which are patent to our senses and the observation of all men, how can we be assured that the remoter blessings we are claiming for the future have any solid foundation? But when we see God come into our present life, and become as real as our misery and sin and as the pains and sicknesses He heals, then we know that our faith for the future is not a dream, but that these things are but the first fruits of the greater blessings of the age to come.

The Lord is a God of infinite benevolence and goodness. . . . Sickness and pain are as foreign to His nature and beneficent will as sin and death. . . . Only a prejudiced and faithless theology could restrict the blessings of His great salvation to mere spiritual blessings and rob a suffering world of the touch of His healing wings.

A. B. Simpson
The Lord for the Body

HYMN FOR TODAY

> *It is to those that fear His name*
> *His healing power the Saviour brings;*
> *Oh, let us hide with contrite hearts*
> *Beneath His healing wings.*
> *Beneath those healing wings I rest,*
> *While all my heart with rapture sings:*
> *The Sun of Righteousness has risen*

With healing in His wings.
"Healing in His Wings"—A. B. Simpson

FRUIT FOR TODAY

The twentieth century Christian has witnessed quantum leaps forward in medical procedures and technology. Once a futuristic theory, the laser beam is now an everyday tool in eye surgery. Transplantation is possible for almost every conceivable part of the human body. Artificial mechanisms are available to replace deficient and diseased members of a person's physiology. Test tube babies are a viable, though controversial, option in reproduction.

Despite all these advances, the most potent and most accessible means for the restoration of physical health is divine healing. If Jesus Christ's ministry to mankind is carefully evaluated, the prominence of healing for the body must be viewed as the most frequent manifestation of His Lordship. He is the Great Physician!

Perhaps we have not because we do not ask! One of the legacies of the holiness movement of the late 19th century is a renewed awareness of God's intervention in the realm of our physical health. Expectations were elevated for healing and wholeness of the body and a revival of divine healing swept over segments of the American church.

Today, why not seek the Lord of the body to meet a physical need which hinders your service to Him!

WEEK SEVEN: Day Seven
Theme: The Pursuit of God

SEED FOR TODAY

As the deer pants for streams of water,
  so my soul pants for you, O God.
My soul thirsts for God, for the living God.
  When can I go and meet with God? (Psalm 42:1-2)

LIGHT FOR TODAY

Christian theology teaches the doctrine of prevenient grace, which briefly stated means this, that before a man can seek God, God must first have sought the man.

Before a sinful man can think a right thought of God, there must have been a work of enlightenment done within him; imperfect it may be, but a true work nonetheless, and the secret cause of all desiring and seeking and praying which may follow.

We pursue God because, and only because, He has first put an urge within us that spurs us to the pursuit. "No man can come to me," said our Lord, "except the Father which hath sent me draw him," and it is by this very prevenient *drawing* that God takes from us every vestige of credit for the act of coming. The impulse to pursue God originates with God, but the out-working of that impulse is our following hard after Him; and all the time we are pursuing Him we are already in His hand. . . .

In this divine "upholding" and human "following" there is no contradiction. All is of God, for as von Hugel teaches, *God is always previous.* In practice, however, (that is, where God's previous working meets man's present response) man must pursue God.

A. W. Tozer
The Pursuit of God

HYMN FOR TODAY

I'm pressing on the upward way,
New heights I'm gaining every day;
Still praying as I onward bound,
"Lord, plant my feet on higher ground."
Lord, lift me up, and let me stand
By faith on heaven's tableland;
A higher plane than I have found,
Lord, plant my feet on higher ground.
     "Higher Ground"--Johnson Oatman Jr.

FRUIT FOR TODAY

"I planted the seed, Apollos watered it, but God made it grow," Paul informed his most troubled church, the church at Corinth (1 Corinthians 3:6). The congregation had moved from the supernatural to the synthetic, arguing about which man they were following.

In Paul's mind they were playing trivial pursuit. Energy and effort were being squandered on "who is the greatest?" Their spiritual leader pointed them to the fact that God is the agent of growth and change. God deserves the glory! God is the indispensable component of any equation.

If the Christian is to grow in grace, he or she must be cognizant that it is because of God's active intervention. Man-made spiritual growth is tailor-made spiritual disaster. God will not share His glory. He is First and Last, He is Author and Finisher, He is Alpha and Omega! This is a marvelous "stress management" exercise, to remember that our God is in control.

Today, give praise to Whom praise is due! And beyond praise, do what God enables you to do. The same Apostle Paul who acknowledged God's sovereignty wrote this autobiographical statement, "I press on toward the goal to win the prize for which God has called me heavenward in Christ Jesus" (Philippians 3:14). The balanced Christian life is both praising God and pursuing God!

WEEK EIGHT: Day One
Theme: The Second Coming

SEED FOR TODAY

And this gospel of the kingdom will be preached in the whole world as a testimony to all nations, and then the end will come. (Matthew 24:14)

LIGHT FOR TODAY

We are preaching the gospel not for the conversion of the world but for a witness unto all nations. When we shall have accomplished this, our Lord will come.

In effect, God has given *us* the key to the future. His great chronometer does not measure time by days and years but by preparations for the marriage of the Lamb and the readiness of the bride. How this should stir us with holy energy and aspiration! I cannot understand how any man or woman can believe in the Lord's coming and not be a missionary—or at least be committed to the work of missions—with every power of his or her being. There is no mockery more sad and inconsistent than for a believer to speak of the blessed hope with folded hands and selfish heart.

No one can rightly believe in the coming of Jesus without expending all the strength of his or her being in preparing for it by sending the gospel to all the nations. God is summoning to a great missionary crusade those who hold this hope today.

A. B. Simpson
Missionary Messages

HYMN FOR TODAY

> *The Master's coming draweth near;*
> *The Son of Man will soon appear;*
> *His kingdom is at hand.*
> *But ere that glorious day can be,*
> *This gospel of the kingdom we*
> *Must preach in every land,*

Must preach in every land.
    "A Missionary Cry"—A. B. Simpson

FRUIT FOR TODAY

The missionary mandate encompasses every disciple of Jesus Christ. No one is exempt from enrollment in the Great Commission campaign!

If you are a person that God has placed in the leadership tier of your local church you can enlarge the "global vision." Please consider lobbying for these elements to be incorporated into your yearly agenda:

1. A *concert of prayer* devoted to missionaries, mission fields, missionary funding and missionary recruitment;

2. A *church budget* which reflects *at least 20 percent* given toward world evangelization;

3. A *short-term missions trip* to an overseas field to assist in the building and renovating of facilities;

4. A *line item in the church budget* for "Scholarship Funds" so that young men and women who have committed their lives to missionary endeavor, and who will need financial support to complete educational requirements prior to departing for a foreign field, will receive adequate support.

Today, you are only one, but your voice may change your church, which may, in turn, shake some region of the world!

WEEK EIGHT: Day Two
Theme: Faith

SEED FOR TODAY

Do not let your hearts be troubled. Trust in God; trust also in me. In my Father's house are many rooms; if it were not so, I would have told you. I am going there to prepare a place for you. And if I go and prepare a place for you, I will come back and take you to be with me that you also may be where I am. (John 14:1-3)

LIGHT FOR TODAY

Faith in Jesus Christ, the right kind of faith, the only kind of faith that matters, is irrevocable, total commitment to the Person of Jesus Christ Himself. You cannot go back on it, and if it is total, there is nothing that is not included. Faith in Jesus is not gulping twice and saying, "I accept Jesus." It is getting into a state where you have totally committed yourself to the Lord Jesus Christ. It is irrevocable commitment to the Person of Jesus Christ.

Faith in Jesus Christ is not commitment to your church or denomination. I believe in the local church; I am not a tabernacle man. I believe in the divine assembly. We ought to realize that we are, as a group of Christians, a divine assembly, a cell in the body of Christ, alive with His life. But not for one second would I try to create in you a faith that would lead you to commit yourself irrevocably to a local church or to your church leaders. . . .

Faith is faith in Jesus Christ, God's Son. It is total faith in Christ and not in a denomination or church, though you may love the church and respect and love your leaders and your denomination. But your commitment is to Christ.

A. W. Tozer
Rut, Rot or Revival

HYMN FOR TODAY

Oft there comes a wondrous message
When my hopes are growing dim,
I can hear it through the darkness
Like some sweet and far-off hymn.
Nothing is too hard for Jesus,
No man can work like Him;
Nothing is too hard for Jesus,
No man can work like Him.
"Nothing Is Too Hard for Jesus"—A. B. Simpson

FRUIT FOR TODAY

Faith has been defined in acrostic form:

Forsaking
All
I
Trust
Him

Christianity does not provide a smorgasbord of options for our faith! He is THE WAY, THE TRUTH AND THE LIFE (John 14:6). The present religious culture emphasizes tolerance and inclusiveness, but Christianity is a very exclusive faith. We should not apologize for this exclusiveness. C.S. Lewis reminded us that 2 + 2 = 4, there is only one *right answer*. The door to salvation is JESUS CHRIST and there are no SIDE ENTRANCES!

The incredible feats of our age prompt us to invest our faith in science, medicine, computer technology, new diets and even in political superstars. History has repeatedly demonstrated that there are always exceptions to the reliability of these and other "bidders" for our faith.

Jesus made His invitation very singular, very exclusive, when He articulated this brief, two-word message, "Follow Me!"

Today, "put your hand in the hand of the Man from Galilee!" It is JESUS ONLY!

WEEK EIGHT: Day Three
Theme: Holiness and Service

SEED FOR TODAY

Then I heard the voice of the Lord saying, "Whom shall I send? And who will go for us?"
And I said, "Here am I. Send me!" (Isaiah 6:8)

LIGHT FOR TODAY

Now, holiness means *separation for service*. The separation is unto God, but the service is for man. Yet all service for man is of course, also service for God. Therefore, sanctification, while a blessed experience, is not an end in itself; it is rather a glorious means to a still more glorious end. This end is a life of fruitful and abiding service alike to God and man. Indeed, we are saved to serve. We are sanctified to minister the riches of divine grace to the sinful and needy.

A holy heart, then, will be an unselfish heart. It will not live for itself, but it will expend its consecrated energies in ready service and in willing sacrifice for others. Again, a holy heart will bear fruit unto God. Fruit is the result of the incoming of the Spirit and the indwelling of Christ. It manifests itself not only in active ministry but also in passive suffering. It includes graces of character as well as records of achievement. Finally, a holy heart will burn with missionary fire. It will have a passion for souls. It will love the lost and seek to win them. Moreover, it will be pressed in spirit toward the regions beyond.

Have you received the Holy Spirit? Have you taken Christ to be your sanctification? Have you had a vision of the world's need? Has there come to you the outward calling? If so, then you are living an unselfish life.

George P. Pardington
The Crisis of the Deeper Life

HYMN FOR TODAY

There are lives that may be brightened by a word of hope
    and cheer,
There are souls with whom life's blessings I should share;
There are hearts that may be lightened of the burdens
    which they bear;
Let me take the blessed hope of the gospel there.
Call me forth to active service,
And my prompt response shall be,

113

"Here am I! Send me.'"
I am ready to report for orders, Master, summon me,
And I'll go on any errand of love for Thee.
"Master, Use Me"—Elisha A. Hoffman

FRUIT FOR TODAY

In Isaiah 6 the student of God's Word records *three* critical observations of the great prophet which rearranged his priorities and redirected his life's journey. He saw the Lord, he saw himself and he saw the world. This sequence purified him and propelled him to be a player not a spectator!

In Matthew 9:37-38 Jesus instructs the disciples to pray for workers to go out into the harvest fields, "Then he said to his disciples, "The harvest is plentiful but the workers are few. Ask the Lord of the harvest, therefore, to send out workers into his harvest field.' " The next verse finds Jesus preparing them to go out! The people praying for workers became the workers! The sign in our one adult Sunday school classroom asked this question, "What is greater than prayer?" I thought about the answer to the interrogative and came up with this response, "When the person praying BECOMES THE ANSWER!" Holiness translates into helpfulness and sanctification leads to service!

Today, grab a towel and "wash someone's feet." Jesus left us with that precedent!

WEEK EIGHT: Day Four
Theme: Divine Healing and Death

SEED FOR TODAY

For to me, to live is Christ and to die is gain. If I am to go on living in the body, this will mean fruitful labor for me. Yet what shall I choose? I do not know! I am torn between the two: I desire to depart and be with Christ, which is better by far. (Philippians 1:21-23)

LIGHT FOR TODAY

The power that brings health or strength to our bodies, or victory to our inner man, is nothing less than the very life of Jesus Christ dwelling in us by His Spirit. The fact of His indwelling life is far more important than the fact of physical healing which results from it. Sooner or later the healing of every human body will cease, but the life of Christ within goes on forever, for "he that is joined to the Lord is one spirit" (I Corinthians 6:17). For this reason we must keep the great truth of divine healing in perspective. At best, it is only a temporary measure, and should be willingly laid aside for the privilege of entering into eternal glory.

In view of all the lip service we Christians give to the glories of heaven, most of us seem strangely reluctant to go there. . . .

Many precious children of God and their families are put into severe bondage and robbed of much blessed fellowship, comfort, and anticipation by struggling to force healing from the hand of God, when God in His love has planned to give them something far better. For many years now, I have discussed this matter of healing versus death with Christians who are afflicted with terminal illnesses. I never take it for granted that God wants to heal them. Maybe He intends to promote them through death into the unspeakable glories of heaven.

Richard Sipley
Understanding Divine Healing

HYMN FOR TODAY

> *When ends life's transient dream,*
> *When death's cold, sullen stream*
> *Shall o'er me roll,*
> *Blest Saviour, then, in love,*
> *Fear and distrust remove;*
> *Oh, bear me safe above,*
> *A ransomed soul!*
>   *"My Faith Looks up to Thee"—Ray Palmer*

FRUIT FOR TODAY

Someone has said, "Everyone wants to get to heaven but no one wants to *die* to get there!" Your death is a divine appointment. Hebrews 9:27 confirms this assertion, "Just as man is destined to die once, and after that to face judgment."

Death for the Christian is a comma not a period. In First Corinthians 15:55, Paul wrote about death in a less than flattering manner, "Where, O death, is your victory? Where, O death, is your sting?"

Jesus, just prior to raising Lazarus from the dead, made this bold proclamation, "I am the resurrection and the life. He who believes in me will live, even though he dies; and whoever lives and believes in me will never die . . ." (John 11:25-26).

Today, remember that the Christian views death and all that accompanies it as a winter season which lead to a springlike resurrection. Death is the doorway to life. Death is the final healing!

WEEK EIGHT: Day Five
Theme: The Indwelling Christ

SEED FOR TODAY

I have been crucified with Christ and I no longer live, but Christ lives in me. The life I live in the body, I live by faith in the Son of God, who loved me and gave himself for me. (Galatians 2:20)

LIGHT FOR TODAY

Our religion is deeper than is commonly supposed. It is a great loss in every way that we are accustomed to speak of faith in Christ, forgiveness, and cleansing from sin as if they were the crown and climax of Christianity, instead of being its outworks, its outer-courts, the staircases and corridors to its throne-room, its reparative processes preparatory to its essential life and heart. Christianity fails its chief end in any life that it affects unless it produces there, so far as may be possible, the life of the Eternal God Himself, as it is resident in Jesus Christ and communicated by the Holy Spirit. . . .

The Lord Jesus is in the heart of each believer by the grace of the Holy Spirit. The perfect image may be in embryo, wrapped up as a forest tree in acorn or seed, but it is certainly present. And each time we are called upon to resemble Christ, to act or speak as He would have done, to reflect Him to men, we have to deal not only with the Christ of the throne, but the Christ of the heart. Let us make way so that the Christ in us may speak or act through us, so that the image without may be reproduced, not simply by reflection, but by indwelling and outshining.

F. B. Meyer
The Glorious Lord

HYMN FOR TODAY

> *Once far from God and dead in sin,*
> *No light my heart could see;*
> *But in God's Word the light I found,*
> *Now Christ liveth in me.*
> *Christ liveth in me,*
> *Christ liveth in me;*
> *Oh, what a salvation this,*
> *That Christ liveth in me!*
> "Christ Liveth in Me"—Daniel W. Whittle

FRUIT FOR TODAY

Abraham Kuyper made this inclusive affirmation: "There is not one inch about which Christ does not say, 'It is mine.'" The Christian life is a replication of Jesus Christ in His followers. The copy is to mirror the Master Copy. You and I are to be conformed to His likeness. There is to be no demarcation in the believer's existence between Jesus Christ and his or her own person. Like a bottle floating in the ocean, the ocean is in the bottle and the bottle is in the ocean.

Today, think on this reality of the New Testament era: Jesus Christ is alive and well inside my inner man. He is changing and rearranging me. I am the clay and He is the potter. Perhaps one day someone will have to take a second look at you as they pass you on the street because, for just a moment, they thought they saw Jesus!

WEEK EIGHT: Day Six
Theme: Temptation

SEED FOR TODAY

To him who is able to keep you from falling and to present you before his glorious presence without fault and with great joy—to the only God our Savior be glory, majesty, power and authority, through Jesus Christ our Lord, before all ages, now and forevermore! Amen. (Jude 1:24-25)

LIGHT FOR TODAY

The English translation is inadequate. The word *falling* means *stumbling*. Of course He is able to keep us from being lost. Too many Christians are content to just get through, if it be by the skin of their teeth. That is a poor, ignoble ambition. He is able to keep us even from stumbling and to present us faultless before the presence of His glory with exceeding joy.

If God is able to keep us for one second, He can keep us for 33 million seconds—one whole year—and as much longer as we keep trusting Him moment by moment. Let us rise to a higher ambition and allow Him to keep us even from slipping, tripping and stumbling. . . .

It is the old familiar picture of the fly on one side of the window and the bird on the other. The bird dashes for its prey and thinks it has it. The fly shudders and thinks so too, but there is a thud and some flustered feathers and a badly frightened bird, but the fly is still there, wondering how he escaped being swallowed up. But to us the secret is all plain: there was something between the bird and the fly that the bird did not see and the fly had forgotten.

Thank God, when the devil makes his fiercest dives, there is Someone between him and us. He has to get through Jesus Christ to get us. If we only abide in simple confidence, the devil will get a good deal more hurt than we.

A. B. Simpson
The Fourfold Gospel

HYMN FOR TODAY

> *Yield not to temptation,*
> *For yielding is sin—*
> *Each victory will help you*
> *Some other to win;*
> *Fight manfully onward,*
> *Dark passions subdue;*
> *Look ever to Jesus,*
> *He will carry you through.*
> *Ask the Saviour to help you,*
> *Comfort, strengthen, and keep you;*
> *He is willing to aid you,*
> *He will carry you through.*
> *"Yield Not to Temptation"—Horatio R. Palmer*

FRUIT FOR TODAY

John Wesley remarked in reference to temptation that you could not stop the birds from flying over your head, but you could stop them from building a nest in your hair. Temptations are inevitable! Their frequency may even escalate after conversion. Our Lord Jesus Christ had Satan's carrot dangled before Him, especially during the initiation of His world-changing ministry and at the climax of His mission as He came to His moment of decision in Gethsemane's garden.

The Bible supplies a powerful promise concerning temptation in First Corinthians 10:13: "No temptation has seized you except what is common to man. And God is faithful; he will not let you be tempted beyond what you can bear. But when you are tempted, he will also provide a way out so that you can stand up under it." This verse assures us that there is an escape hatch for every temptation we encounter!

Today, when the tempter comes knocking at your door, practice the presence of God, who will enable you to resist and repel the overtures of your opponent! *Standing*, not *falling*, is the order of the day!

WEEK EIGHT: Day Seven
Theme: Resist the Devil

SEED FOR TODAY

Submit yourselves, then, to God. Resist the devil, and he will flee from you. (James 4:7)

LIGHT FOR TODAY

But Satan is an old dragon who defies us to this hour. He is saying to Christians, "I defy you—what can you do about it?"

I think we had better get free! We must face up to the issues and attitudes and doubts which constitute our fears, that keep us from being happy and victorious Christians with the true liberty of the children of God. We seem to quake about many things.

In the first place, are you still afraid of your past sins? God knows that sin is a terrible thing—and the devil knows it, too. So he follows us around and as long as we will permit it, he will taunt us about our past sins.

As for myself, I have learned to talk back to him on this score. I say, "Yes, Devil, sin is terrible—but I remind you that I got it from you! And I remind you, Devil, that everything good—forgiveness and cleansing and blessing—everything that is good I have freely received from Jesus Christ!"

Everything that is bad and that is against me I got from the devil—so why should he have the effrontery and brass to argue with me about it? Yet he will do it because he is the devil, and he is committed to keeping God's children shut up in a little cage, their wings clipped so that they can never fly!

A. W. Tozer
I Talk Back to the Devil

HYMN FOR TODAY

Arise, my soul, arise!
Shake off thy guilty fears;
The bleeding Sacrifice
In my behalf appears.
Before the throne my Surety stands,
Before the throne my Surety stands:
My name is written on His hands.
"Arise, My Soul, Arise!"—Charles Wesley

FRUIT FOR TODAY

C.S. Lewis warned the church in *The Screwtape Letters* that believers are vulnerable when they spend too much time focusing on the devil. Every child of God should *respect* him, but it is more critical to *resist* him. Satan is a prince, but Jesus is a King!

Today, don't allow the devil to put a lid on you. As the divine life of Christ flows through you, there is a dynamic that exceeds the devil's capabilities. John shared this principle of the Christian life in a tiny letter that carries a big bang in spiritual warfare: "You, dear children, are from God and have overcome them, because the one who is in you is greater than the one who is in the world" (1 John 4:4).

WEEK NINE: Day One
Theme: Practical Sanctification

SEED FOR TODAY

I am the vine; you are the branches. If a man remains in me and I in him, he will bear much fruit; apart from me you can do nothing. If anyone does not remain in me, he is like a branch that is thrown away and withers; such branches are picked up, thrown into the fire and burned. If you remain in me and my words remain in you, ask whatever you wish, and it will be given you. This is to my Father's glory, that you bear much fruit, showing yourselves to be my disciples. (John 15:5-8)

LIGHT FOR TODAY

There are certain practical steps by which this life of sanctification is lived out day by day.

1. We are to live a life of implicit obedience to God, doing always what He bids and being wholly under His direction.

2. We are to be obedient to His voice. We will need to listen closely for Jesus speaks softly.

3. In every time of conflict or temptation or testing, we are to draw near to God and give the matter over to Him. Instead of the sweet and happy experience you would naturally expect after such a consecration, the devil comes and tries to shake your confidence by some trial or temptation. Stand in Him and rejoice that He counts you worthy to receive such trials. If you fail, don't say it is no use to try further. The principle is right. Perhaps you tried to do the work yourself and so you failed. Stop and lay it all at His feet and start afresh, and learn to abide in Him from your very failure.

Israel, after her defeat at Ai, was stronger for the next conflict. Try to live out the secret you have learned. In human art there is always stumbling at first. You can learn the principles of stenography in a very little while, a few hours perhaps, but it takes months of patient practice to become expert at it.

The moment we are consecrated to Jesus Christ we learn the secret that He is to be all-in-all to us. But when we try to practice this truth, we find that it takes time and patience to learn it thoroughly. We must learn to lean on Him. We must learn little by little how to take Him for every need.

A. B. Simpson
The Fourfold Gospel

HYMN FOR TODAY

Make me a captive, Lord,
And then I shall be free;
Force me to render up my sword,
And I shall conqueror be.
I sink in life's alarms
When by myself I stand;
Imprison me within Thine arms,
And strong shall be my hand.
　　"Make Me a Captive, Lord"—George Matheson

FRUIT FOR TODAY

One of the most heralded New Testament Greek scholars in this century made this assessment, "Perfect Practice Makes Perfect." The general maxim is that "practice makes perfect," but Professor Metzger took it up a notch. There will be spills even for the sanctified, but each success as well as each failure has a part in conforming a believer to the image of Jesus Christ.

The theology of sanctification embraces *crisis* (a moment of filling) and *process* (a lifetime of growing). Christ is the Sanctifier, which means that He is the Potter and we are the clay. The disciple is not able to manufacture a sanctified life without the Sanctifier. However, the believer can determine how fast and how far the process moves by his or her willingness to allow Jesus to pilot the ship and not just be the passenger.

Today, a temptation or test will confront you. Program yourself through prayer to pause and request that Jesus Christ guide your response through His Holy Spirit! As you practice this response to life's tests your scores will inevitably curve upward!

WEEK NINE: Day Two
Theme: Sanctification

SEED FOR TODAY

What, then, shall we say in response to this? If God is for us, who can be against us? He who did not spare his own Son, but gave him up for us all—how will he not also, along with him, graciously give us all things? (Romans 8:31-32)

LIGHT FOR TODAY

"Is there not something better than this life of sin and failure? Is there not as much power in our Christ to keep us now as there will be some day to glorify us in heaven beyond?" . . .

Sanctification is not a garment to conceal unrighteousness. It is not a veneering to hide a life spiritually untransformed. Sanctification means renewed character and righteous conduct. It involves a radical revolution in personality. There is a change in the temper of the mind, in the disposition of the heart and in the bent of the will. But the blessing of a clean heart is inseparable from the possession of the clean heart by the Holy Ghost. Without His presence the cleansing of the temple would not be permanent. Sanctification is not ours apart from the person of Christ. We are holy only as we are in vital union with the Holy One. When we get *Him*, we get *everything* in Him. . . .

Thus our watchword for a holy life and a fruitful ministry is: "Everything in Jesus, and Jesus everything."

George P. Pardington
The Crisis of the Deeper Life

HYMN FOR TODAY

Jesus, my Saviour, is all things to me,
Oh, what a wonderful
Saviour is He;
Guiding, protecting, o'er life's rolling sea,
Mighty deliverer—Jesus for me.
Jesus for me, Jesus for me,
All the time, everywhere,
Jesus for me!
"Jesus for Me"—William J. Kirkpatrick

FRUIT FOR TODAY

Herbert Schlossberg, in his book, *Idols for Destruction*, made this painful assessment: "Protestantism has largely divested itself of the transcendent and has become almost indistinguishable from the surrounding culture." Rather than standing out, the contemporary church, and by reduction, the contemporary Christian, easily blends into the environment. The Old Testament and New Testament canonical records find this situation unacceptable. Whether it was the Israelites compared to the Canaanites, or the Roman Christians lined up next to the unbelievers of the Empire, the result was to be visible contrast.

Men and women of the faith are desperately needed whose morality reflects God's holiness, whose light shines in darkness, whose fragrance permeates a stench-filled room, whose lives are a *counterculture* to a world which operates from a non-theistic ethic! It was Rowland Hill who wrote: "I would give nothing for that man's religion whose very dog and cat are not the better for it." The old but still relevant question is: "If you and I were arrested for being a Christian, would there be enough evidence to convict us?"

Today, determine to be a counterculture Christian!

WEEK NINE: Day Three
Theme: The Holy Spirit

SEED FOR TODAY

Where can I go from your Spirit?
  Where can I flee from your presence?
If I go up to the heavens, you are there;
  if I make my bed in the depths, you are there.
If I rise on the wings of the dawn,
  if I settle on the far side of the sea,
even there your hand will guide me,
  your right hand will hold me fast. (Psalm 139:7-10)

LIGHT FOR TODAY

The Holy Spirit is not only a Person, but . . . a divine Person; not only a divine Person, but God.

In Psalm 139 the hymnist attributes omnipresence to the Holy Ghost . . . and he develops throughout the 139th Psalm, in language that is as beautiful as a sunrise and as musical as the wind through the willows, the idea that the Spirit is everywhere, having the attributes of deity. He must be deity, for no creature could have the attributes of deity.

In Hebrews (9:14) there is attributed to the Holy Ghost that which is never attributed to an archangel, or a cherubim, or an angel, or a patriarch, or anyone that has ever been created by the hand of God. It says, "Through the eternal Spirit," and every theologian knows that eternity is an attribute of no creature which deity has ever formed. The angels are not eternal; that is they had a beginning, and all created things had beginning. As soon as the word "eternal" is used about a being it immediately establishes the fact that he never had a beginning, is not a creature at all, but God. Therefore, when the Holy Ghost says "the eternal Spirit" about Himself He is calling Himself God.

A.W. Tozer
How to Be Filled with the
Holy Spirit

HYMN FOR TODAY

Holy Spirit, all divine,
Dwell within this heart of mine;
Cast down every idol throne;
Reign supreme—and reign alone.
    "Holy Ghost, with Light Divine"—Andrew Reed

FRUIT FOR TODAY

Fred Hartley articulates a concise and fundamental statement on the Holy Spirit in *Prayer Voices*:

> As we get to know the Holy Spirit, perhaps the most important thing we need to learn about Him is that He is a *Person*. Far more than simply being a power or impersonal force, He is just as much a real live, distinct person as you and I.

God values socialization, the interaction and interfacing of persons. The creation account notes only one dissatisfaction with the original creative acts of God: "The LORD God said, 'It is not good for the man to be alone. I will make a helper suitable for him'" (Genesis 2:18).

God socializes with the creatures of His making through the Person of the Holy Spirit. He has guaranteed that the nexus between the Divine and the human species will be concrete, not abstract; personal, not impersonal.

Today, have a personal, intimate discussion with God's personal agent, the Holy Spirit!

WEEK NINE: Day Four
Theme: Love

SEED FOR TODAY

We love because he first loved us. If anyone says, "I love God,"
yet hates his brother, he is a liar. For anyone who does not love
his brother, whom he has seen, cannot love God, whom he has not
seen. And he has given us this command: Whoever loves God must
also love his brother. (1 John 4:19-21)

LIGHT FOR TODAY

The love of Christ both wounds and heals, it fascinates and
frightens, it kills and makes alive, it draws and repulses. There
can be nothing more terrible or wonderful than to be stricken
with love for Christ so deeply that the whole being goes out in a
pained adoration of His person, an adoration that disturbs and
disconcerts while it purges and satisfies and relaxes the deep inner
heart.

This love as a kind of moral fragrance is ever detected upon the
garments of the saints. In the writings of Augustine, Bishop of
Hippo, for instance, this fragrance is so strong as to be nearly
intoxicating. There are passages in his *Confessions* so passionately
sweet as to be unbearable, yet so respectful and self-effacing as to
excite pity for the man who thus kneels in adoring wonder, caught
between holy love and an equally holy fear.

The list of fragrant saints is long. It includes men and women of
every shade of theological thought within the bounds of orthodox
Christian faith. It embraces persons of every social level, every
degree of education, every race and color. This radiant love for
Christ is to my mind the true test of catholicity, the one sure proof
of membership in the church universal.

A. W. Tozer
That Incredible Christian

HYMN FOR TODAY

My Jesus, I love Thee, I know Thou art mine,
For Thee all the follies of sin I resign;
My gracious Redeemer, my Saviour art Thou,
If ever I loved Thee, my Jesus, 'tis now.
   "My Jesus, I Love Thee"—William R. Featherstone

FRUIT FOR TODAY

Jesus Christ has left His church a legacy of *first love*. He did not react to our love; rather, He made the initial move of reconciliation—even though we were sinners, He sacrificed His life for us (Romans 5:8).

Today, be sensitive to someone who does not possess strong affection or affinity for you. Exercise first love toward that individual. Pray that this person will be fertile soil for Christlike love. You may be surprised by the reaction. The woman at the well and two tax collectors named Zacchaeus and Matthew, among others, were transformed by first love. Perhaps your target will be touched today.

Will your diary tomorrow include an entry of Christlike, proactive first love?

WEEK NINE: Day Five
Theme: Enlargement

SEED FOR TODAY

Enlarge the place of your tent,
   stretch your tent curtains wide,
   do not hold back;
lengthen your cords,
   strengthen your stakes. (Isaiah 54:2)

LIGHT FOR TODAY

God's plan for His work involves taking the weak and immature person and developing him or her to maturity. Using this mature Christian, He then multiplies His work, and the process starts again in another person. The work He has done for us is but a sample of what He can do and wants to do for all the world. The blessing that has filled and thrilled our hearts may be multiplied as many times as there are cities in the world. It can be reproduced wherever there are hungry hearts to fill and messengers to tell of the grace and fullness of Jesus. That humble work, which has grown up out of a "handful of corn on the top of the mountains," can become a mighty forest on all the mountains. It can "flourish like Lebanon" or "thrive like the grass of the field" (Psalm 72:16).

God has been making samples, but He can multiply them by the millions. Will we let Him use us for their reproduction? That is how they are multiplied. They are not manufactured like machines in a factory. They grow as seeds grow—like the oak by the acorns it drops into the ground or like the single grain of wheat that sometimes sends up 20 stalks from a single seed, each stalk bearing half a hundred more seeds.

God has given us a gospel so full that it needs a world for its field.

A. B. Simpson
A Larger Christian Life

HYMN FOR TODAY

So, amid the conflict, whether great or small,
Do not be disheartened—God is over all;
Count your many blessings, angels will attend,
Help and comfort give you to your journey's end.
Count your blessings, name them one by one;
Count your blessings see what God hath done!
Count your blessings, name them one by one;
Count your many blessings, see what God hath done.
     "Count Your Blessings"—Johnson Oatman Jr.

FRUIT FOR TODAY

"Anyone can count the seeds in an apple, but only God can count the apples in one seed." Are you that seed, small but mighty if multiplied and amplified? The redwood seed is 1/16th of an inch long but produces a tree 12 feet in diameter and 300 feet high. Don't discount your impact on this world! You are only one, but you are one and you can make a dramatic difference. One plus God makes an incredible sum!

"But God chose the foolish things of the world to shame the wise; God chose the weak things of the world to shame the strong," Paul states in First Corinthians 1:27. Moses spoke these words to the children of Israel on the east side of the Jordan, "For you are a people holy to the LORD your God. The LORD your God has chosen you out of all the peoples on the face of the earth to be his people, his treasured possession. The LORD did not set his affection on you and choose you because you were more numerous than other peoples, for you were the *fewest* of all peoples" (Deuteronomy 7:6-7).

Today, our God has the inclination and intention to choose the weak to manifest His strength, to select the small and then do incredible feats. If you are aware of your deficiencies, beware—God may choose you, because then He will get the credit!

WEEK NINE: *Day Six*
Theme: Worship

SEED FOR TODAY

He put a new song in my mouth,
  a hymn of praise to our God.
Many will see and fear
  and put their trust in the LORD. (Psalm 40:3)

LIGHT FOR TODAY

The treacherous enemy facing the church of Jesus Christ today is the dictatorship of the routine, when the routine becomes "lord" in the life of the church. Programs are organized and the prevailing conditions are accepted as normal. Anyone can predict next Sunday's service and what will happen. This seems to be the most deadly threat in the church today. When we come to the place where everything can be predicted and nobody expects anything unusual from God, we are in a rut. The routine dictates and we can tell not only what will happen next Sunday, but what will occur next month, and, if things do not improve, what will take place next year. Then we have reached the place where what has been determines what is, and what is determines what will be.

That would be perfectly all right and proper for a cemetery. Nobody expects a cemetery to do anything but conform. The greatest conformists in the world today are those who sleep out in the community cemetery. They do not bother anyone. They just lie there, and it is perfectly all right for them to do so. You can predict what everyone will do in a cemetery from the deceased right down to the people who attend a funeral there. Everyone and everything in a cemetery has accepted the routine. Nobody expects anything out of those buried in a cemetery. But the church is not a cemetery and we should expect much from it, because what has been should not be lord to tell us what is, and what is should not be ruler to tell us what will be. God's people are supposed to grow.

A.W. Tozer
Rut, Rot or Revival

HYMN FOR TODAY

Joyful, joyful we adore Thee,
God of glory, Lord of love;
Hearts unfold like flowers before Thee,
Opening to the sun above.
Melt the clouds of sin and sadness,
Drive the dark of doubt away;

Giver of immortal gladness,
Fill us with the light of day.
        "Joyful, Joyful, We Adore Thee"—Henry Van Dyke

FRUIT FOR TODAY

It might be time for some new ingredients to be added to the recipe of your life. The dictatorship of the routine can become stale and stifling. A change may elevate your level of expectation and it may help you discover some untapped resources in your life.

There are many ways you can modify your routine. If you are a pastor, why not restructure your week and take a different day off for restoration? If you have input into your church's worship format, consider adding a new instrument or singing a stanza a cappella or rearranging the worship sequence. What about your daily devotions? There is a wide assortment of devotional helps available to enhance your quiet time with the Lord. When was the last time you redecorated your office or kitchen? Plant some different flowers in the yard this spring!

Today, don't be a gerbil in a cage just running in circles. Changing your environment is a choice. Break the bondage of routine!

WEEK NINE: Day Seven
Theme: Authority of the Believer

SEED FOR TODAY

I pray also that the eyes of your heart may be enlightened in order that you may know the hope to which he has called you, the riches of his glorious inheritance in the saints, and his incomparably great power for us who believe. That power is like the working of his mighty strength, which he exerted in Christ when he raised him from the dead and seated him at his right hand in the heavenly realms, far above all rule and authority, power and dominion, and every title that can be given, not only in the present age but also in the one to come. (Ephesians 1:18-21)

LIGHT FOR TODAY

Authority, then, is delegated power. Its value depends upon the force behind the user. There is a story told of the Right Honorable W. E. Gladstone, when he served as Prime Minister of Great Britain. On one occasion, he brought in to Queen Victoria, an important measure for her signature, in order that it might become law. The queen objected to it, and after some discussion, refused to sign. The Minister of the Crown was unusually urgent: "Your majesty," he said, respectfully but firmly, "You must sign this Bill." She turned on him haughtily: "Sir, I am the *Queen* of England." Unmoved, the statesman answered quietly, "Your Majesty, I am the *people* of England." After a little thought, she accepted the situation, and affixed her signature to the document.

This story may be apocryphal, but it illustrates the question of authority when two opposing powers are in conflict. The believer, who is fully conscious of divine Power behind him, and of his own authority thereby, can face the enemy without fear or hesitation. Those who confront him bear the specific names of power and authority: "we wrestle not against flesh and blood, but against principalities [*archas*, the first or preeminent ones], against powers [*exousias*, the authorities]." But, behind the "authority" possessed by the believer, there is a "Power" infinitely greater than that which backs his enemies, and which they are compelled to recognize.

John A. MacMillan
The Authority of the Believer

HYMN FOR TODAY

Stand up, stand up for Jesus,
Ye soldiers of the cross;
Lift high His royal banner,
It must not suffer loss.
From victory unto victory

His army shall He lead,
Till every foe is vanquished
And Christ is Lord indeed.
      "Stand Up, Stand Up for Jesus"—George Duffield

FRUIT FOR TODAY

Ephesians 6 details the wardrobe of the believer who encounters opposition in spiritual warfare. The elements of this suit of armor and weaponry include:

truth (6:14)	faith (6:16)
righteousness (6:14)	salvation (6:17)
readiness (6:15)	Word of God (6:17)

The tyranny of the urgent often prevents the contemporary Christian soldier from properly dressing for battle. Billy Graham said that the epitaph of our age would read "Hurry, Worry, Bury."

Today, are you rushing into the conflict without proper spiritual nutrition and discipline? Daily devotions are a necessity for "getting dressed." The components of the battle garb are "put on" by prayer, praise and a daily encounter with God's Word. Don't forget to get dressed. Your authority can be traced to your times of interaction with the Ultimate Authority, the Commander-in-Chief, Jesus Christ!

WEEK TEN: Day One
Theme: Leadership

SEED FOR TODAY

Have I not commanded you? Be strong and courageous. Do not be terrified; do not be discouraged, for the LORD your God will be with you wherever you go. (Joshua 1:9)

LIGHT FOR TODAY

The future of the church of Jesus Christ is in heaven. For the present, though, God is building it in human history. That building is a process that spans centuries and has a cumulative character to it.

Because of this, the battle line in one generation is not always the scene of greatest conflict in another. There is ebb and flow. That does not change the fact, however, that what is at the forefront of discovery in one generation may be assumed in another. The process is dynamic. Thus, what is creatively revolutionary in one age may seem almost trite, if not sterile, in another.

Consequently, the church is in continual need of those souls who can discern where the crucial issues are in their day and can devote their energies to providing leadership in these areas. There will always be those intent upon reinventing the wheel, i.e., rewinning battles already won. These individuals are of minimal significance to the movement of God's Spirit in history. Some hardy souls occasionally get beyond the front line. Their isolation, however, reduces their effectiveness. The sensitive soul who perceives the moment's crucial issues and gives guidance in dealing with them is the prophetic figure that every generation needs. Albert Benjamin Simpson (founder of The Christian and Missionary Alliance) was such a person.

Dennis Kinlaw
The Birth of a Vision

HYMN FOR TODAY

Lead on, O King eternal,
The day of march has come;
Henceforth in fields of conquest
Thy tents shall be our home.
Through days of preparation
Thy grace has made us strong,
And now, O King eternal,
We lift our battle song.

   "Lead On, O King Eternal"—Ernest W. Shurtleff

FRUIT FOR TODAY

In every definable era of church history, God has placed men and women equipped with the qualities of leadership. The Old Testament brings to remembrance men such as Abraham, Moses, Joshua and David. Women such as Deborah and Esther seized the moment of their nation's historical struggles. The New Testament features many personalities including Mary, Peter and Paul.

The Christian church has, since New Testament times, been enriched by church fathers such as Augustine, martyrs such as Polycarp, reformers such as Luther and Calvin, revivalists such as Wesley, Whitefield, Finney and Graham.

These hardy souls looked over the ridge of human history and led others to new heights and horizons. You may not lead a grand movement in church history, but you may be one of the men and women God calls to be frontrunners in government, education or medicine. He has planted many of us in the local church and in our family units so that the way may be clearly marked and the risks may be taken to insure that God's will is accomplished in the basic institutions of our society and culture.

Someone has stated, "We are one generation away from extinction."

Today, intercede for leaders, those in the prominent and influential sectors of society. Also, assess where God has positioned you and be open to those opportunities which inevitably come to all of us, to step forward and take a leadership role.

WEEK TEN: Day Two
Theme: Lordship

SEED FOR TODAY

Then Peter began to speak: "I now realize how true it is that God does not show favoritism but accepts men from every nation who fear him and do what is right. You know the message God sent to the people of Israel, telling the good news of peace through Jesus Christ, who is Lord of all. (Acts 10:34-36)

LIGHT FOR TODAY

All living things need a ruling force. The body is useless, and immediately plays the fool, without a head to direct its movements. An army is powerless when there is no supreme commander to issue orders. The finest vessel ever launched is certain to strike upon the rocks unless there is a captain on the bridge. There is certain to be anarchy in the family if the father forgets that he is the husband, or house-band.

If these things are true in the lower realms, how much more important is the question of authority when we speak of our relation to our Lord. A true Christian is a man or woman under the authority of the Lord Jesus Christ. His crown rights, as Lord of all, are not dependent on our recognition of them. They were the Father's gift to the Beloved Son for His great mediatorial work. . . .

The name "Lord" is seldom found even in the Gospels. The Apostle John uses it because it was given to him to point men to the Son of God in all the glory of His relation to the Father, as the Lord Jesus Christ. It occurs frequently in the Acts of the Apostles, for the Church was to be built historically upon this magnificent truth: "Know assuredly," said Peter, "that God hath made that same Jesus, whom ye have crucified, both Lord and Christ" (Acts 2:36).

J. Gregory Mantle
The Counterfeit Christ

HYMN FOR TODAY

Standing on the promises of Christ the Lord,
Bound to Him eternally by love's strong cord,
Overcoming daily with the Spirit's sword,
Standing on the promises of God.
Standing, standing,
Standing on the promises of God, my Saviour;
Standing, standing,
I'm standing on the promises of God.
"Standing on the Promises"—Russell K. Carter

FRUIT FOR TODAY

The civil rights movement of the 1950s and 60s had an immeasurable impact on American culture. The individual who had been restricted because of discrimination was liberated and permitted to exercise new freedoms and capitalize on new opportunities. These "rights" were tantamount to a new sovereignty in human endeavor.

The "rights" question is now an epidemic issue—it is raised by virtually every group in society. There are placards waving for women's rights, children's rights, gay rights, Indian rights and even animal rights. The believer detects a down side in this avalanche of rights rhetoric and activism. When Jesus becomes Lord, a man or woman surrenders all rights on the table. The issue of His Lordship is non-negotiable! This is the way but it chafes many who consider the Christian message and is a sizeable irritant for multitudes who have obeyed Jesus' command to "follow Me."

Today, reaffirm the Lordship of Jesus Christ in your life, in every dimension, in every endeavor of your existence. Be sensitive today for a time when you make Him sovereign in a moment of personal choice. He is Lord *of* all, or He is not Lord *at* all!

WEEK TEN: Day Three
Theme: Revival

SEED FOR TODAY

Search me, O God, and know my heart;
* test me and know my anxious thoughts.*
See if there is any offensive way in me,
* and lead me in the way everlasting. (Psalm 139:23-24)*

LIGHT FOR TODAY

When people in the church only point to others for improvement and not to themselves, it is sure evidence that the church has come to dry rot. It is proof of three sins: the sin of self-righteousness, the sin of judgement and the sin of complacency.

When our Lord said, "One of you will betray me," thank God those disciples had enough spirituality that nobody said, "Lord, is it he?" Every one of those disciples said, "Lord, is it I?" If they would not have so responded there could not have been a Pentecost. But because they were humble enough to point the finger in their own direction the Holy Spirit fell upon them.

Self-righteousness is terrible among God's people. If we feel that we are what we ought to be, then we will remain what we are. We will not look for any change or improvement in our lives. This will quite naturally lead us to judge everyone by what we are. This is the judgment of which we must be careful. To judge others by ourselves is to create havoc in the local assembly.

Self-righteousness also leads to complacency. Complacency is a great sin and covers just about everything I have said about the rote and the rut. Some have the attitude, "Lord, I'm satisfied with my spiritual condition. I hope one of these days You will come, I will be taken up to meet You in the air and I will rule over five cities." These people cannot rule over their own houses and families, but they expect to rule over five cities. They pray spottily and sparsely, rarely attending prayer meeting, but they read their Bibles and expect to go zooming off into the blue yonder and join the Lord in the triumph of victorious saints.

A. W. Tozer
Rut, Rot or Revival

HYMN FOR TODAY

Search me, O God, search me and know my heart;
Try me and prove me in the hidden part;
Cleanse me and make me holy, as Thou art,
And lead me in the way everlasting.
Lead me, lead me, lead me in the way everlasting;
Keep me from things that wither and decay;
Give to me the things that cannot pass away—
And lead me in the way everlasting.
   "Search Me, O God"—A. B. Simpson

FRUIT FOR TODAY

In his book, *Healing the Dysfunctional Church Family*, David
Mains casts this warning:

> Research shows that dysfunctional families are charac-
> terized by unhealthy comparisons and even outright com-
> petition. "I'm smarter (or prettier or more athletic or
> better at making money) than you are. Just compare
> houses (or cars or jobs or wardrobes) and you'll see!"
> But what kind of a family is that? The experts would say
> it is a sick family.

Someone has asserted, "It takes no size to criticize!" There is
always someone a little bit more sinful or a little less holy. The
bedrock appeal to God is not "Search them" but "Search me."

Today, have a personal "board meeting" with yourself. Call the
meeting to order with David's prayer from Psalm 139 (see SEED FOR
TODAY). Take up "old business" and submit to your heavenly Father
a list of things that need to be resolved. Petition Him to endow you
with the discernment to handle the "new business" that awaits you.

This type of self-examination is biblical and it results in a vessel that the Holy Spirit can flow through unimpeded by sin, stain or impediment.

WEEK TEN: Day Four
Theme: Forgetting Myself

SEED FOR TODAY
He must become greater; I must become less. (John 3:30)

LIGHT FOR TODAY

God never can use any man very much till he has grace enough to forget himself entirely while doing God's work; for He will not give His glory to another nor share with the most valued instrument the praise that belongs to Jesus Christ alone.

We can never succeed in our service for God till we learn to cast our own shadow behind us and lose ourselves in the honor and glory of our Master. It is said that Alexander the Great had a famous horse that nobody could ride. Alexander at length attempted to tame him. He saw at a glance that the horse was afraid of his own shadow, and so, leaping into the saddle one day and turning the horse's head to the sun, he struck his spurs into the flanks of the noble steed, and dashed off like the lightning. From that hour the fiery charger was thoroughly subdued, and he never gave his master any trouble again. He could no longer see his own shadow.

Oh, that we could look into the face of our Lord, and then forever forget ourselves! Then He could use us for His own glory and afford to share with us the glory and gladness of our work.

A. B. Simpson
The Self-Life and the Christ-Life

HYMN FOR TODAY

Not I but Christ be honored, loved, exalted;
Not I but Christ be seen, be known, be heard;
Not I but Christ in every look and action;
Not I but Christ in every thought and word.
Oh, to be saved from myself, dear Lord!
Oh, to be lost in Thee!
Oh, that it might be no more I,
but Christ that lives in me!
    "Not I, But Christ"—A. A. Whiddington

FRUIT FOR TODAY

The Christian life produces a counterculture lifestyle. You live in a society which encourages you to pamper yourself and promote your choices as sovereign. There are egomaniacs running around in some Christian communities and ministries. The name of the man or the title of the group supersedes the signature of the Lord Jesus Christ. If you listen to some people, their song is not "I Exalt Thee," but "I Exalt Me!" Following Jesus will escalate one's servanthood and diminish one's self-promotion and self-aggrandizement.

Charles Swindoll described the three major periods of Moses' life in these terms: "Moses spent his first forty years thinking he was somebody, his middle years learning he was nobody, and his later years discovering what mighty deeds God could perform through a nobody." The self life had to be subjugated in order that this man could manifest the life of God within him before the great empire of Egypt and before the people he would lead out of captivity, the Israelites.

Today, strive to promote God and His greatness. Strive to refrain from tooting your own trumpet. The venerated Puritan saint Thomas Hooker, as he prepared to die, was surrounded by many who stood vigil. The remark was made, "Brother Hooker, you are going to receive your reward."

"No, No!" he responded, "I go to receive mercy." He had cultivated the art of forgetting himself!

WEEK TEN: Day Five
Theme: Risks

SEED FOR TODAY

Then Esther sent this reply to Mordecai: "Go, gather together all the Jews who are in Susa, and fast for me. Do not eat or drink for three days, night or day. I and my maids will fast as you do. When this is done, I will go to the king, even though it is against the law. And if I perish, I perish." (Esther 4:15-16)

LIGHT FOR TODAY

Isn't it good to be involved in something bigger than ourselves. And to be into something which is so formidable and so challenging that all we can say as we gurgle going down, "Save me, Lord, or I perish." This living dangerously . . . is a great thing. It is great to be alive at such a time as this. . . .

Because men . . . took risks, we are here today. But in the history of organizations, those that are often started at the greatest risk become the kind of organizations in time who are not willing and able to take the smallest kind of risk. We seem to give birth to our opposite in time, so now we are called to a renewal of our earliest commitments in taking on our tasks for the world.

It was a vibrant church in Antioch—because they were people who were not super-saturated with the Word of God. They were people who were not just inventorying truth but people who were day-by-day incorporating the truth of God into positive action. They were doing what they were supposed to be doing and people were coming to the Lord. And, of course, they were challenged in many ways. . . . Our people, if anything, are under-challenged, looking for a cause that involves some kind of risk, needing some place to express their love to Christ in a sacrificial way.

David Rambo
As Many As Possible

HYMN FOR TODAY

Would you in His kingdom find a place of constant rest?
Would you prove Him true in providential test?
Would you in His service labor always at your best?
Let Him have His way with thee.
His power can make you what you ought to be;
His blood can cleanse your heart and make you free;
His love can fill your soul and you will see
'Twas best for Him to have His way with thee.
        "Would You Live for Jesus?"—Cyrus S. Nusbaum

FRUIT FOR TODAY

When was the last time you rode a swing set and knew that your feet couldn't touch the ground? When was the last time you climbed into thin air? How long has it been since you swam in deep water?

Impact people make the journey into new frontiers because they believe that their extremity is God's opportunity! If you play it safe, you don't need an awesome God. Your goals and dreams do not demand His involvement.

Today, start visualizing a project which necessitates the assistance of HEAVEN! Release your grip on the trunk of the tree and venture out where the branches are thin!

Reflect on Ephesians 3:20: "Now to him who is able to do immeasurably more than all we ask or imagine, according to his power that is at work within us," and begin to actively pursue some miraculous adventures in your life—yes, *your* life. Risks are often righteous endeavors!

WEEK TEN: Day Six
Theme: Highway of Holiness

SEED FOR TODAY

May God himself, the God of peace, sanctify you through and through. May your whole spirit, soul and body be kept blameless at the coming of our Lord Jesus Christ. The one who calls you is faithful and he will do it. (1 Thessalonians 5:23-24)

LIGHT FOR TODAY

How easy, how spontaneous, how delightful this heavenly way of holiness! Surely it is a "highway" and not the low way of man's vain and fruitless mortification. It is God's great elevated railway, sweeping over the heads of the struggling throngs who toil along the lower pavement when they might be borne along on His ascension pathway, by His own Almighty impulse. It is God's great elevator, carrying us up to the higher chambers of His palace without our laborious efforts, while others struggle up the winding stairs and faint by the way. It is God's great tidal wave bearing up the stranded ship until she floats above the bar without straining timbers or struggling seamen, instead of the ineffectual and toilsome efforts of the struggling crew and the strain of the engines, which had tried in vain to move her an inch until that heavenly impulse lifted her by its own attraction. It is God's great law of gravitation lifting up, by the way of sunbeams, the mighty iceberg which a million men could not raise a single inch, but which melts away before the warmth of the sunshine and rises in clouds of evaporation to meet its embrace until that cold and heavy mass is floating in fleecy clouds of glory in the blue ocean of the sky.

How easy all this! How mighty! How simple! How divine! Beloved, have you come into the divine way of holiness? If you have, how your heart must swell with gratitude as it echoes the truths of the words you have just read! If you have not, do you not long for it and will you not now unite in the prayer of our text that the very God of peace will sanctify you wholly?

A. B. Simpson
Wholly Sanctified

HYMN FOR TODAY

Jesus is our Sanctifier,

Cleansing us from self and sin,
And with all His Spirit's fullness,
Filling all our hearts within.
Jesus only, Jesus ever,
Jesus all in all we sing,
Saviour, Sanctifier, and Healer,
Glorious Lord and coming King.
            "Jesus Only"—A. B. Simpson

FRUIT FOR TODAY

A. W. Tozer reminded readers in *I Talk Back to the Devil* that, "the word mediocre comes from two Latin words and literally means 'halfway to the peak.' " Sanctification is the experience which empowers the saved person to reach the peak. It is a spiritual landmark which offers a clearer view, a spiritual plateau which positions one on higher ground.

Not everyone aspires to higher ground. Some will be content in the dry and dusty lowlands of the Christian journey. Others will begin the ascent to higher ground but will stall along the climb. But to those who open their lives up to God's fullness, who allow the Holy Spirit to chart and lead their ascent, their diary will record that they stood tall on the peak of praise and power!

Today, where will you stand, in the lowlands, at the halfway marker, or will you plant your feet where the view is breathtaking on higher ground?

WEEK TEN: Day Seven
Theme: The Second Coming

SEED FOR TODAY

After he said this, he was taken up before their very eyes, and a cloud hid him from their sight.

They were looking intently up into the sky as he was going, when suddenly two men dressed in white stood beside them. "Men of Galilee," they said, "why do you stand here looking into the sky? This same Jesus, who has been taken from you into heaven, will come back in the same way you have seen him go into heaven." (Acts 1:9-11)

LIGHT FOR TODAY

Only the Christian church in the midst of all the world's religions is able to proclaim the Bible's good news that God, the Creator and Redeemer, will bring a new order into being!

Indeed, it is the only good news available to a fallen race today—the news that God has promised a new order that is to be of eternal duration and infused with eternal life.

How amazing!

It is a promise from God of a new order to be based upon the qualities which are the exact opposite of man's universal blight—temporality and mortality!

God promises the qualities of perfection and eternity which cannot now be found in mankind anywhere on this earth.

What a prospect!

We are instructed that this new order, at God's bidding, will finally show itself in the new heaven and the new earth. It will show itself in the city that is to come down as a bride adorned for her husband.

The Word of God tells us that all of this provision for the redeemed has the quality of eternal duration.

It is not going to come just to go again. It is not to be temporal. It is a new order that will come to stay.

It is not going to come subject to death. It is not to be mortal. It is a new order that will come to live and remain forever!

A. W. Tozer
Tragedy in the Church:
The Missing Gifts

HYMN FOR TODAY

Marvelous message we bring,
Glorious carol we sing,
Wonderful word of the King—
Jesus is coming again!
Coming again, Coming again;
Maybe morning, maybe noon,
Maybe evening and maybe soon!
Coming again, Coming again;
Oh, what a wonderful day it will be—
Jesus is coming again!
  "Jesus Is Coming Again"—John W. Peterson

FRUIT FOR TODAY

In *Rabbi Ben Ezra*, Robert Browning wrote this famous phrase, "The best is yet to be." The authentic Christian could adopt this as a motto. The "dice of life" are loaded! The Lord of history is in control! The end has been known from the beginning. Revelation 11:15 shows a preview of coming attractions: "The seventh angel sounded his trumpet, and there were loud voices in heaven, which said: 'The kingdom of the world has become the kingdom of our Lord and of his Christ, and he will reign for ever and ever.' "

Jesus is coming again! And if death comes for you before our precious Lord, remember, death is only for a moment—*life* is forever. Death is not the final act, death is only intermission. Death is not a period, just a comma. Reflect upon Jesus' words as He stood at Lazarus' tomb: "Jesus said to her, 'I am the resurrection and the life. He who believes in me will live, even though he dies; and whoever lives and believes in me will never die' " (John 11:25-26).

At His coming, the living and dead in Christ will be fused into one grand universal church! Listen to the climactic words of First Thessalonians 4:16-18: "For the Lord himself will come down from heaven, with a loud command, with the voice of the archangel and with the trumpet call of God, and the dead in Christ will rise first. After that, we who are still alive and are left will be caught up together with them in the clouds to meet the Lord in the air. And so we will be with the Lord forever. Therefore encourage each other with these words."

Today, rejoice! *The best is yet to be!*

Scripture Index

Author Biographies

Bailey, Keith

A retired Christian and Missionary Alliance pastor and former district superintendent in the Ohio Valley, Keith Bailey is also the author of several books, including *The Children's Bread, Christ's Coming and His Kingdom* and *Servants in Charge*.

Cowles, H. Robert

The former executive vice president of Christian Publications, and editor of *Alliance Life* magazine, H. Robert Cowles, who also served as a missionary to the Philippines, is the author of a number of books, including *Opening the New Testament, Opening the Old Testament* and *Prime Time*.

Davey, James E.

Pastor James Davey is the author of *The Riches of Grace*.

Foster, K. Neill

The executive vice president/publisher of Christian Publications and a noted evangelist, Neill Foster has written such books as *The Discerning Christian, The Happen Stance, The Third View of Tongues* and *Dam Break in Georgia*.

Francis, R. Mabel

R. Mabel Francis was a missionary to Japan and the author of *Filled with the Spirit . . . Then What?* and *One Shall Chase a Thousand*.

Gesswein, Armin R.

Armin Gesswein is the founder and director of the Revival Prayer Fellowship, Inc., and the Ministers' Prayer Fellowship. The long-time revival preacher is the author of *With One Accord in One Place*.

Hunter, J.H.

Besides being a journalist and editor, J.H. Hunter was the author of *Beside All Waters*, which is out of print.*

Jacobs, Joy

When God Seems Far Away, They Were Women, Too and *They Were Women Like Me* are all books written by Joy Jacobs, who is a popular conference speaker as well as an author.

Jaffray, Robert

A pioneer missionary statesman to Southeast Asia, Robert Jaffray was editor of *The Pioneer*. His biography, *Let My People Go*, by A.W. Tozer is still in print.

King, L. L.

L.L. King is both the former president of The Christian Missionary and Alliance and a former missionary to India.

Kinlaw, Dennis

Dennis Kinlaw, a popular conference speaker, was a former president of Asbury College.

MacMillan, John A.

John MacMillan was not only a missionary, pastor, teacher and editor, but also the author of *The Authority of the Believer* and *Encounter with Darkness*.

Mantle, J. Gregory

J. Gregory Mantle was a theologian and author of *The Counterfeit Christ*.

Meyer, F.B.

F.B. Meyer was a preacher, expositor and author of *The Glorious Lord*, no longer in print.

Nelson, Wyman

Wyman Nelson is a missionary to Burkina Faso.

Pardington, George P.

George Pardington was a theologian and the author of *The Crisis of the Deeper Life* and *Outline Studies in Christian Doctrine.*

Rader, Paul

Paul Rader was a former president of The Christian and Missionary Alliance Church and the author of *God's Blessed Man,* now out of print.

Rambo, David

Dr. David Rambo is currently the president of The Christian and Missionary Alliance. He has also been a missionary and president of Nyack College.

Roberts, Donald L.

Donald L. Roberts is a pastor and author of *The Practicing Church.*

Shepson, Charles W.

Charles Shepson is a pastor, a gifted counselor and author of *How to Know God's Will* and *A Heart for Imbabura.*

Simpson, Albert Benjamin

Although perhaps best known as the founder of The Christian and Missionary Alliance, A.B. Simpson was much more. In addition to launching a great missionary movement, he was a conference speaker and evangelist whose fervor for God's kingdom led him to the masses in New York City. His hymns and the 42 books of his which remain in print pass on his rich spiritual legacy.

Sipley, Richard

Conference speaker and pastor Richard Sipley is the author of *Understanding Divine Healing.*

Stebbins, Thomas

Not only a missionary, pastor, professor and trainer for the Evangelism Explosion program, Thomas Stebbins is also the author of *Evangelism by the Book.*

Stoesz, Samuel J.

Retired pastor and professor, Samuel Stoesz is also the author of *Sanctification: An Alliance Distinctive, Church and Membership Awareness* and several other books which are now out of print.

Sutherland, Spence

Spence Sutherland is a former missionary to Vietnam who now works with Vietnamese district of The Christian and Missionary Alliance in the United States.

Tam, Stanley

Stanley Tam is a businessman and author of *God Owns My Business* and *God's Woodshed*.

Taylor, Delores

Delores Taylor is the author of *Women in God's Presence*.

Tozer, Aiden Wilson

Author of over 40 books in print, pastor of Southside Alliance Church in Chicago for 31 years, and editor of *Alliance Life* until his death in 1963, A.W. Tozer was dedicated to God's call. His messages, interwoven with mystic and prophetic threads, were sometimes biting but always powerful and serious. *The Pursuit of God* is probably his best-known book.

Wardle, Terry Howard

Terry Wardle is a pastor, educator and author of *Exalt Him!*, *Wounded* and *One to One*.

Westergren, Cliff

Cliff Westergren is currently using his missionary experience as administrator and director for Alliance CAMA Services.

The following books quoted from in *Planted by the Water* are still published by Christian Publications and may be ordered through your local Christian bookstore or by calling 1-800-233-4443.

The Authority of the Believer	MacMillan, John A.
Born After Midnight,	Tozer, A.W.
The Children's Bread	Bailey, Keith
The Crisis of the Deeper Life	Pardington, George P.
Days of Heaven on Earth	Simpson, A.B.
The Discerning Christian	Foster, K. Neill
Exalt Him!	Wardle, Terry H.
Evangelism by the Book	Stebbins, Thomas
Filled with the Spirit . . . Then What?	Francis, R. Mabel
The Fourfold Gospel	Simpson, A.B.
God Owns My Business	Tam, Stanley
How to Be Filled with the Holy Spirit	Tozer, A.W.
How to Know God's Will	Shepson, Charles W.
I Call It Heresy!	Tozer, A.W.
I Talk Back to the Devil	Tozer, A.W.
A Larger Christian Life	Simpson, A.B.
The Life of Prayer	Simpson, A.B.
Missionary Messages	Simpson, A.B.
Prime Time, 366 Devotions for Seniors	Cowles, H. Robert
The Pursuit of God	Tozer, A.W.
Rut, Rot or Revival	Tozer, A.W.
Sanctification: An Alliance Distinctive	Stoesz, Samuel J.
The Self-Life and the Christ-Life	Simpson, A.B.
That Incredible Christian	Tozer, A.W.
Tragedy in the Church: The Missing Gifts	Tozer, A.W.
Understanding Divine Healing	Sipley, Richard
When the Comforter Came	Simpson, A.B.
Wholly Sanctified	Simpson, A.B.
Women in God's Presence	Taylor, Delores